SPEEDING INTO ACTION: THE INFLUENCE OF PARAMILITARY CULTURE ON DISASTER RESPONSE ORGANIZATIONS IN THE 2010 HAITI EARTHQUAKE

Jeffrey D. Stern

Dissertation submitted to the faculty of Virginia Polytechnic Institute and State University in partial fulfillment of the requirements for the degree of

Doctor of Philosophy
In
Public Administration/Public Affairs
Center for Public Administration and Policy
School of Public and International Affairs

Patrick S. Roberts, Committee Chair
Anne M. Khademian
Matthew Dull
James F. Wolf

Fall 2014
Alexandria, Virginia

Keywords: Haiti earthquake, disaster response, paramilitary, FEMA, Coast Guard, SOUTHCOM

Speeding into Action: the Influence of Paramilitary Culture on Disaster Response
Organizations in the 2010 Haiti Earthquake

ABSTRACT

This dissertation examines the influence of paramilitary professional cultural
attributes on the speed at which disaster response organizations (DROs) recognize, respond,
organize, and take action in the immediate aftermath of a disaster. Three agencies are
examined: the U.S. Coast Guard, the Federal Emergency Management Agency, and the U.S.
military's Southern Command/Joint Task Force-Haiti. The 2010 Haiti earthquake is used as
a case study to explore the influence of three independent variables: (1) paramilitarism; (2)
career ladders (i.e., recruitment and professional development of staff); and (3) workforce
autonomy. The purpose is to determine if paramilitary cultures help or hinder an agency's
speed into action, thereby helping improve the disaster response organizations of the future.
In the case of Haiti, it finds that the combination of thick paramilitary culture, insider career
ladders, and high workforce autonomy best enabled responders' speed into action.

TABLE OF CONTENTS

LIST OF FIGURES

LIST OF TABLES

DEDICATION

This work is dedicated to those who go into harm's way to put order to chaos -- to heal, to help, and to provide hope. May the organizations that send them enable success, and not inhibit their capabilities to serve, save, and lift the spirits of the survivors of acts of both God and man. This is for you all, with thanks.

I am grateful to those who have inspired me to continue this work over the past decade, from family and friends, fellow students, and colleagues: you all are too numerous to thank individually. Every single one of you helped me continue this effort. I owe a great deal to professional friends who have passed this Ph.D. Rubicon before, and reached back to give me advice or encouragement when needed: Drs. Bob Griffin, Charles Jennings, Jen Jacobs, Matt Fleming, Michele Malvesti, Dan Kaniewski, Ron Clark, Clay McGuyer, Amy Donahue, Gerry Cox, and Jason Dean. Thanks also to Nick Stone and my colleagues at the VT Arlington Research Center where I finished this research and writing.

I must acknowledge my friends from the Operational Medicine Institute and Beth Israel Deaconess Medical Center with whom I had the privilege of serving in the Dominican Republic and Haiti after the earthquake in 2010. That experience directly inspired the selection of this case.

A special thanks to my committee members: Anne Khademian, who always had just the right amount of advice to propel me forward; Matt Dull, who served as a great sounding board and provided some key direction at critical times; Jim Wolf, my initial chair and professor emeritus, whose experience always brought a dose of reality necessary to right-size my aspirations; and Patrick Roberts, whose arrival and assumption of the chair upon Jim's retirement helped me reinvigorate and refine my proposal and take these final steps.

My parents inspired my lifelong pursuit of knowledge; for that gift I am also grateful. JJ, marrying an ABD has not been easy; and I would not have completed this without your love, encouragement, and sacrifice of time together.

This project endeavors to capture the essence of the heroic efforts to save the people of Haiti after the 2010 earthquake. To save one life is to save the world.

CHAPTER I. CHARGE!

"Where in the hell is the cavalry on this one? We need food. We need water. We need people. For God's sake, where are they?"
-*Kate Hale, Dade County Emergency Manager, in the wake of Hurricane Andrew* (Wamsley 1996).

"The cavalry arrives, but refugees and local officials want to know why it took so long."
-*AP News Headline after Hurricane Katrina, September 3, 2005* (Tanner 2005).

"I'm not going to sit around again and wait for the cavalry to get here."
-*New Orleans Mayor Ray Nagin, commenting on new city evacuation plans* (CNN 2005).

"U.S. Marines SOS. We need help."
- *Homemade sign in front of a collapsed building, Port-au-Prince, Haiti (Roig-Franzia 2010).*

The arrival of the cavalry to the rescue is an iconic American image, indelibly burned into the minds of everyone around the world who has ever seen a classic John Ford Hollywood Western movie. It is this image of the chivalrous rescuers, the sounds of bugles and thundering hooves, a cloud of dust growing large on the horizon, and John Wayne leading the charge that comes to mind the instant someone mentions the word "cavalry".

When disasters strike around the globe, this image is reinforced and becomes part of our common jargon. We watch the news and see the U.S. Navy and Marines providing aid to tsunami victims in the Pacific Rim, we see columns of U.S. Army troops roll into New Orleans to rescue people from the Superdome, and we see tons of American aid airlifted and then dropped into devastated regions of Pakistan or Haiti after an earthquake. During catastrophes, the image of the cavalry coming to the rescue is never far from our thoughts.

The cavalry's arrival serves as a metaphor for government's response to disasters. As a metaphor, the image of response is not just likened to the arrival of the cavalry, it actually becomes the arrival of the cavalry: something visceral, reinforced, and imprinted on our minds by all those old movies, and used for years in the common jargon and language we apply to descriptions of disaster response. The cavalry riding to the rescue is a metaphor -- perhaps the single most powerful metaphor -- that describes public expectations and perceptions about the role of government in catastrophes. This metaphor holds whether we are describing the wail of the siren from a city's red fire engine, the blinking of the strobe lights from a state trooper's police car, or the rumbling sound of a column of National Guard troop carriers: it is a metaphor applied equally to domestic and international emergency response.

Such was the expectation when a catastrophic earthquake struck Haiti on January 12, 2010, as local survivors called for the U.S military to help (Roig-Franzia 2010). The earthquake registered 7.0 on the Richter scale, the scientific chart that measures the strength of the shifting earth on a scale between 1.0 and 10.0 (U.S. Geological Survey 2013). The quake's epicenter was near to Port-au-Prince, the Haitian capital and population center. Thousands of buildings collapsed. Hundreds of thousands of Haitians were injured and an estimated 100,000 to 300,000 people were killed (Weisenfeld 2011). Figure 1 illustrates the earthquake intensity and the movement of survivors away from the epicenter (Operation Unified Response 2010, 11).

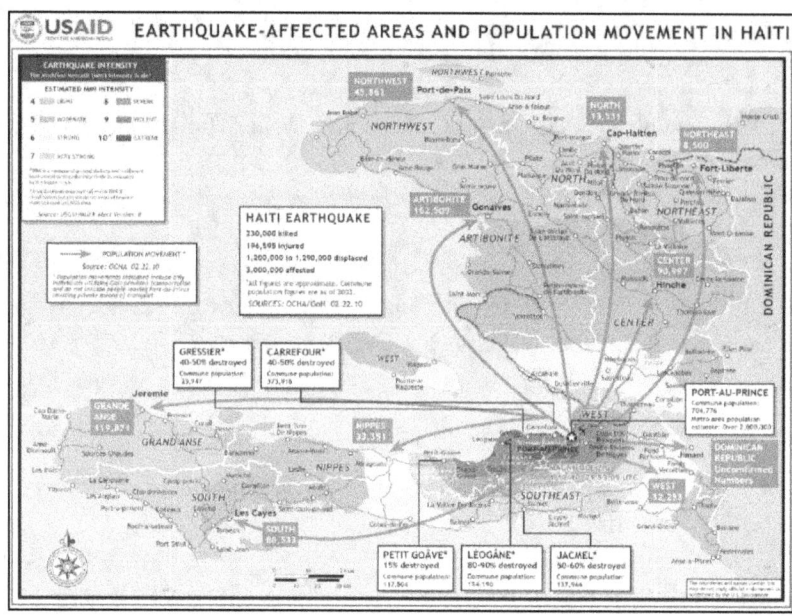

Figure 1. EARTHQUAKE AFFECTED AREAS IN HAITI, 2010 (Operation Unified Response 2010, 11).

A sovereign nation with a long history of poverty and poor governance, Haiti was not prepared to handle the crisis. At the time of the 2010 earthquake, the Haitian government was led by President René Préval. It was his second time serving as President of Haiti. With his government in disarray after the earthquake, there was no cavalry to for Préval to summon.

Haiti remains the poorest country in the Western hemisphere (CIA 2013). Seventy-six percent of the population lives on $2 or less per day (Stephenson and Zanotti 2012). Prior to the 2010 earthquake, Port-au-Prince had a population of 1.7 million people, with a population density of 73,000 people per square mile; by comparison, New York City has a density of 26,000 people per square mile. The city was impoverished and crowded. Beyond the capital, Haiti has an additional 9 million people; the vast majority is poor and illiterate. French and French Creole are the primary languages (CIA 2013).

Haiti has faced political turmoil for most of its history. From 1957 until to 1986, Haiti was a dictatorship, first under Francois "Papa Doc" Duvalier and later under his son, Jean-Claude "Baby Doc" Duvalier. In subsequent years Haiti underwent a series of transitional governments and military coup d'états (CIA 2013). Years of dictatorship and turmoil left behind weak government institutions and weak national leadership.

Haiti shares the island of Hispaniola with the Dominican Republic (DR). The Dominicans and the Haitians have a long, strained history that begins with a Dominican revolt in 1844, during which they won independence from Haiti. The longstanding dislike between the Haitians and the Dominicans made the DR reluctant to send its cavalry to the rescue; they would adopt a minimal posture to support their island neighbors, and remained worried that many Haitians would pour across the border as refugees.[1]

Haiti has relied on outside institutions for many decades. Many international organizations have attempted to address the historical governance and poverty issues in Haiti. Hundreds of small and large non-governmental organizations (NGOs) provide healthcare, education, housing, and other services for Haiti's poorest citizens (Muggah 2010, Zanotti 2010).

In addition to the NGOs, the United Nations has kept a military presence since 2004 with its peacekeeping forces, having established and maintained the United Nations Stabilization Mission in Haiti (MINUSTAH) (United Nations Mission 2013).[2] MINUSTAH maintained a force of 9,065 personnel; 7,031 were military forces and 2,034 were police (Stephenson and Zanotti 2012). Finally, prior to the earthquake, the U.S. military had a long history in Haiti, deploying forces many times between 1888 and 2010, most recently for peacekeeping operations in 2008.[3] However, many of the United Nations leaders in Haiti were killed in the quake, including its top two diplomatic officials.

As a security group, the U.N.'s peacekeeper force wasn't designed for, nor was it capable of, mounting an organized response to the immediate catastrophe. The Haitian government was also "paralyzed and traumatized" (Bhattacharjee and Lossio 2011, 20). That left the majority of the work to the United States and its disaster response organizations. These organizations included all the U.S. military agencies, civilian agencies like the U.S. Agency for International Development (USAID) and the Federal Emergency Management Agency (FEMA), and humanitarian non-governmental organizations (NGOs) like the Red Cross (RC). Between 500 and 1,000 NGOs helped in the aftermath of the earthquake (Ryan 2010; Mandeles 2010). This work examines the efforts of several of these responding agencies, focusing on the distinction between their military and civilian organizational attributes.

THE COMMAND-OR-COORDINATE PROBLEM & RESEARCH QUESTION

In the disaster management literature, the military approach to disaster relief, referred often as the "command and control" model, has been generally disfavored, in preference for a networked "coordination" approach (Waugh 2006). The command model is seen as top-down, hierarchical, and slow to respond, requiring a singular leader to control response actions, while coordination has been viewed as a flexible approach fitting an ethos shared among many humanitarian organizations that seek to help survivors without hierarchical control structures, direction, or lines of authority and control. However, military forces often make up the vanguard of disaster response, supported and followed by diverse civilian and non-governmental organizations. The public cries out for the cavalry.

This dissertation seeks to further examine this issue by looking at the influence of paramilitary culture on disaster response organizations, in an effort to determine how

---

[1] Author's personal observations in Haiti during the response to the earthquake, January-February 2010.
[2] MINUSTAH is the French acronym for *Mission Des Nations Unies Pour La Stabilisation En Haïti.*
[3] The U.S. military has undertaken many operations in Haiti. They are: 2010, Unified Response; 2008, Continuing Promise; 2005, New Horizons; 2004, Secure Tomorrow; 1994, Uphold Democracy; 1994, Restore Democracy; 1915, U.S. Occupation; 1914, U.S. Interventions; 1889, Navassa Island Incident; 1888, U.S. Show of Force (Global Security 2013).

variations might have influenced an organization's speed to recognize, respond, organize, and act in the immediate aftermath of catastrophe. It seeks to answer the research question, *how did paramilitary culture influence the speed into action of disaster response organizations during the initial response to the Haiti earthquake?* While there have been many other disasters that could have been selected, Haiti is a recent catastrophe.[4] The nation of Haiti is still recovering from this disaster. Importantly, as an international event in which President Obama commanded a "whole of government" response, Haiti provides a "neutral" playing field to look at the organizations' performances, unlike domestic emergencies in which roles and responsibilities for disaster response are more clearly defined in legislation and doctrine (through the Stafford Act and the *National Response Framework*, for example).[5]

Building organizations that can respond successfully to disasters is important. The failed response to Hurricane Katrina undermined American's confidence in their government, the President's reputation, America's image around the world, and most importantly, led to the deaths of between 1,300 and 1,800 people in 2005 (Rubin 2012; Olsen 2010; Boin et al 2010, 707). Nearly 300,000 people perished in the Haiti earthquake in 2010 (Bhattacharjee and Lossio 2010). Clearly, both lives and reputations are at stake.

For this research, three independent variables have been chosen to examine these paramilitary cultural attributes. The three variables include (1) the DRO's career ladder, as evidenced through the selection and professional development of staff from either inside or outside the organization; (2) the "thickness" of paramilitarism in each DRO, as evidenced by the presence of cultural symbols and formal organizational processes; and (3) the autonomy of DRO workers based upon type of workforce culture in the organization. The organizations selected for this study are disaster response organizations involved in the first two weeks after the disaster occurred: the U.S. Coast Guard (USCG), the Federal Emergency Management Agency (FEMA), and the U.S. military (focusing specifically on the actions of Southern Command (SOUTHCOM) and its Joint Task Force - Haiti (JTF-Haiti), which led the military response). In doing so, it endeavors to illuminate a greater understanding of disaster response organizations, and further explore aspects of the command/control and coordination paradigms. This research has implications for DROs in designing future professional development programs, and for other organizations that seek to develop a fast-acting, effective, and expeditionary disaster response capability.

---

[4] While some emergency management literature distinguishes between the terms "disaster" and "catastrophe", they are used interchangeably in this paper. Gary Kreps and Thomas Drabek have described several ways of defining the term disaster, summarizing disasters as "non-routine social problems" (Kreps 1995, Kreps and Drabek 1996).

[5] The "whole of government" terminology was first used in the U.S. at the beginning of the Obama administration to describe a cross-agency approach to a variety of wicked policy problems. Like many recent public sector initiatives (e.g. New Pubic Management), the concept is drawn from British and New Zealand public sector reforms effort started as early as 1997. See Christensen and Laegreid (2006) for an overview. In the U.S., whole of government was heavily advocated by the Project for National Security Reform.

CHAPTER II. RESEARCH DESIGN

This section describes the research framework used in this dissertation, including a discussion of the dependent variable (speed into action) and the independent variables (paramilitarism, career ladders, and workforce autonomy). The use of the methodologies of a case study and process tracing are discussed, along with sources of data (including literature, government documents, and interviews of members of selected disaster response organizations).

DEPENDENT VARIABLE: SPEEDING INTO ACTION

Disaster response organizations are relied upon to provide essential services in the wake of both natural and man-made emergencies. In the response phase of an unfolding catastrophe, these essential services might include command and coordination; logistics; administration and finance services; search, rescue and lifesaving operations such as medical care, feeding, and sheltering survivors; and operational planning. Federal guidance for disaster response has evolved over the past decade, from a federal-centric view as written into the early *Federal Response Plan* and *National Response Plan* of the 1979-2005 FEMA-era, to the more recent efforts to guide and integrate state and local response as seen in post-Katrina revisions to the *National Response Framework* (FEMA 2008). In the Obama administration, this evolution is seen in the emphasis on "whole community" response in *Presidential Policy Directive 8: National Preparedness* (Obama 2011).[6]

Over the past several decades there has been research on disasters, organizations, and organizational culture; however, there is less research on how specific organizational cultures influence disaster response organizations, especially on their ability to recognize, respond, organize, and act during catastrophes. The Disaster Research Center, for example, conducted many field studies of disasters (Quarantelli 1982). Organizations must recognize a crisis has occurred, respond with resources to address pressing needs, organize those resources into a system that effectively, efficiently and equitably coordinates aid efforts. The concept of sensemaking, for example, has been researched to study how individuals and organizations recognize extraordinary, non-routine situations, as was show in Weick's seminal work on a wildfire crew, and recently by Boin and Renaud in relation the development of a common operating picture of a catastrophic event (Weick 1993, Boin and Renaud 2013). Responding quickly is critical; according to the United Nations:

> Much of the loss of life during a hazard event occurs in the first 24-48 hours. Maximising [sic] the speed and efficiency of the response effort, and particularly of search and rescue teams, in this initial phase is critical (United Nations 2008, 32).

---

[6] "Whole Community" is FEMA's reinterpretation of the "Whole of Government approaches discussed in Chapter 1. It accounts for non-governmental entities, as well as citizens and private organizations.

Much work has been done to improve the organization of response efforts: in the U.S., for example, disaster response is organized around the National Incident Management System (NIMS), a modular system for organizing that divides responders into "command" and "general" staffs (FEMA 2008).

The influence of paramilitary culture on diverse organizations tasked with carrying out various disaster response activities is the focus of this dissertation. It endeavors to contribute to the nexus between several areas of scholarship, fitting at the intersection of the literature of public administration, organization culture, and disaster management. The four processes of recognition, response, organization, and action are measured here under the overarching idea of speed. Since the DROs do not exist on equal footing, like racehorses at a starting gate, but instead start on patrol, on watch, or in some other routine of organizational activity, speed is not meant to present a specific measure of time, but a more general race against the clock to begin and sustain response activities. For example, FEMA personnel carry on many routine functions such as training or exercising in between disaster responses, while the U.S. Coast Guard might be on a security patrol. The cavalry is not necessarily mustered and ready for action when something bad happens. Table 1 illustrates how these key phases are used to observe how an organization recognizes, responds, organizes, and takes action. Speed is more than just a time factor, but the ability to effectively and efficiently cycle through these four key phases. In this speed to action lives are saved.

Action	Outcome Measure
Recognize	• Aware something bad is happening • Accurate with problem (understanding) • Time to alert
Respond	• Authorization to respond • Time to deploy
Organize	• Time to set up, integrate, or establish network. • Time organizational structure established
Activity	• Time to begin "doing something that needs to be done" • All-needed resources on scene to conduct initial actions

Table 1. SPEEDING INTO ACTION

Why Speed is Important

There is something critical about the first days of a catastrophe. It is where we respond to answer human needs, or where we fail and a sense of anomie takes hold. Hurricane Andrew and Katrina serve as exemplars of response failure; Hurricane Sandy and the Pentagon 9/11 responses are cited as exemplars of response success (Wamsley 1996, Townsend 2006, FEMA 2013, Leonard 2004). During Andrew and Katrina, FEMA was generally viewed as bumbling, slow, and unresponsive to urgent needs. Congressman Norman Mineta said FEMA, "could screw up a two car parade" (Farazmand 2001, 378). It was during Hurricane Andrew that Dade County Emergency Manager Kate Hale uttered her infamous quote, "Where in the hell is the cavalry on this one? We need food. We need water. We need people. For God's sake, where are they?" (Wamsley 1996). In contrast, the collaborative efforts of the fire department, police department, and the military in response to the attack on the Pentagon at 9/11 are widely considered a best practice and kept the fires from eliminating the Pentagon's command and control functions (Leonard 2004, Creed and Newman 2008).

Disasters are also increasing in their economic, social, and human toll. The United Nations determined that direct economic losses from disasters so far this century are 50 percent higher than previous estimates, approaching $2.5 trillion (UN *Global Assessment Report on Disaster Risk Reduction* 2013). In the U.S. alone, the National Climate Data Center has stated that natural disasters resulted in over $110 billion in costs in 2012 (NOAA 2013). United Nation's data indicated that 1.2 million people have been killed in disasters in the past 12 years, as show in Figure 2 (UN *Disaster Impact* 2013). Poor populations are especially vulnerable: Haiti had long been known as "near the bottom" of the U.N. disaster risk index (National Research Council 2007, 138). The earthquake in Haiti is estimated to have cost at least $8.1 billion USD (Cavallo et al 2010).

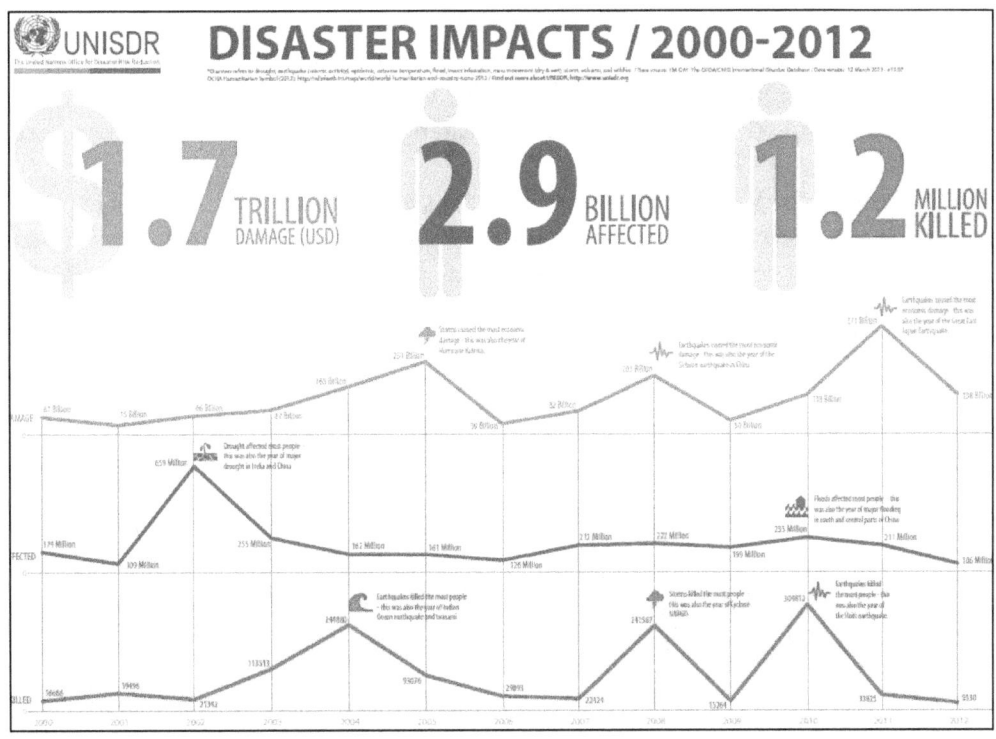

Figure 2. DISASTER IMPACTS 2000-2012 (UNISDR 2013).

After a disaster occurs, we rely on various organizations to respond. Some are government organizations, like the Federal Emergency Management Agency; some are military organizations, like the National Guard or U.S. Navy. Others are non-governmental organizations, like the Red Cross. Some are hybrids, like the U.S. Coast Guard, which has both military and nonmilitary missions (USCG 2009).

Failure to effectively respond to a disaster has undermined the reputation of some DROs (as FEMA has found out in repeated fashion); failure also results in additional, avoidable deaths and suffering, and undermines trust in government. For example, the 9/11 attacks broke confidence in the U.S. counterterrorism regime, leading to reforms at the Federal Bureau of Investigation, the creation of the Department of Homeland Security, and the prosecution of two wars (9/11 Commission 2002). Hurricane Katrina undermined confidence the federal government's ability to handle a predicable catastrophe, led to the firing of an agency leader, and undermined confidence in American governance, eventually leading to the Post Katrina Emergency Management Reform Act (U.S. House of Representatives 2006, Rubin 2012). Therefore, a study of the particular organizing contexts and culture in a DRO is relevant and will contribute to the fields of public administration, organizational culture, and disaster management.

Disaster response organizations have different methods of organizing. These range from decentralized, networked humanitarian organizations like the Red Cross, or government agencies with civilian governance structures like FEMA or the USAID's Office of Foreign Disaster Assistance (OFDA), to traditional, hierarchical, and centralized military structures as found in the U.S. Coast Guard, the National Guard Bureau, and other military forces like the U.S. Army or U.S. Navy. For example, the National Guard, as a military organization, has a clearly delineated military hierarchy. Its soldiers and airmen (or women) are indoctrinated through an initial training course, known as "boot camp", and there is a distinct separation of responsibility between the officer corps and the enlisted troops. The same is true of other military organizations like the Navy, Army, Marines, Air Force, and Coast Guard. FEMA, on the other hand, does not have a distinct indoctrination for all employees, and the role definitions between managerial positions and line positions are blurred.

Despite their differences, these organizations are all tasked -- indeed all expected -- to recognize when something bad is happening, to rapidly respond, to organize and marshal their resources, and to act to do some sort of good, whether rescuing survivors or delivering aid and comfort. They are expected to ride to the rescue. So in addition to saving lives, it is in this "speed into action" that organizational success or failure also is often decided. The military's Joint Center for Operational Analysis (JCOA) conducted a review of disaster response operations, finding its first and primary lesson that:

> Speed of response is the most critical element of successful HADR [humanitarian assistance disaster response] operations. The ability to move people, equipment, and supplies not only to, but throughout, the operational area determines, in most cases, whether the operation is a success. In HADR operations, the speed of initial response is more critical than efficiency (JCOA 2011, 1).

The military's role in disaster response has been the subject of some study. The role of the National Guard in emergency management, for example, was given much attention by the National Academy for Public Administration (Wamsley 1997). That report found that the Guard is "a definite asset if part of an effective planned and coordinated state emergency management system" (Wamsley 1997, xii). This study also specifically pointed to the challenge of filling the "zone of ambiguity" that exists when a disaster has immediately occurred, the roles and responsibilities have not yet been established, and there is "...time and political pressures on decision-makers, coupled with a resulting tendency to override established procedures" (Wamsley 1997, xiv).

While FEMA, the U.S. military, and the U.S. Coast Guard have been studied as individual organizations, there is little comparative work examining the difference between these organizations. Assessing variations between these organizations might provide some insight into the positive and negative influence of certain organizational characteristics, for example, the hierarchy used in military organizations such as SOUTHCOM, or the decentralization of organizations such as FEMA, which is divided into 10 semi-autonomous regions. Since speed into action is important (both to save lives and, it seems, to save organizations' reputations), understanding how these factors influence the ability to recognize, respond, organize, and take action may be of value.

INDEPENDENT VARIABLES: CAREER LADDERS, PARAMILITARISM, AND WORKFORCE AUTONOMY

Three independent variables have been selected for examination in DROs and speed into action: career ladders, paramilitarism, and workforce autonomy. First, *what is the career ladder in the organization, as depicted through its professional recruitment and development?* Is it an organization like the military where there is a defined career ladder that starts at the bottom of the organization, or is it a model where members can enter at any given level, at almost any given time, like the Red Cross or FEMA? The baseline will be to establish whether the organization recruits its staff at the entry levels, and internally develops and promotes them, or whether it has an external focus, and recruits or promotes from outside the organization. SOUTHCOM and the Coast Guard might provide examples of the former model, and FEMA of the latter. Therefore, this variable can be characterized as either an "insider" oriented organization, or an "outsider" oriented organization (reflecting the common jargon used in hiring process: e.g., "they hired an insider"). This distinction between insiders and outsiders might have influence on the organizations stability, culture, innovation, or on employee relationships and experience.

Second, *what impact does the level of paramilitarism have on these organizations?* Is there a difference between having a military culture or a civilian culture in how fast the disaster response organization moves in these early stages? This variable can be characterized in each organization as either a "thick" or "thin" paramilitary culture. Will thicker paramilitary cultures lead to faster response, because of an action bias among members, or will it inhibit response, because military personnel refuse to mobilize without orders from a centralized hierarchy? During Hurricane Katrina, for example, some have criticized the speed at which the military was able to mobilize: "The issue that has attracted the most attention in post-Katrina discussions has been the speed of rescue and relief operations. Northern Command began its alert and coordination procedures before Katrina's landfall; however, many deployments did not reach the affected area until days later" (Bowmen et al 2006).

Third, *how does the workforce autonomy influence these organizations?* Do the members have a lot of latitude and autonomy, as professions tend to have, or are there many administrative or managerial controls on the work that needs to get done in the aftermath of a disaster, reflective of a bureaucratic culture with less autonomy? Table 2 outlines the framework that is proposed.

Independent Variables		
Career Ladder	Insider	Outsider
Paramilitarism	Thick	Thin
Workforce Autonomy	High	Low

Table 2. INDEPENDENT VARIABLES INFLUENCING SPEED TO ACTION FOR DISASTER RESPONSE ORGANIZATIONS.

METHODOLOGY: A CASE STUDY

This dissertation reviews literature and government documents, and employs interviews to gather data related to DROs and the Haiti crisis. Qualitative case study methodology can employ observations to test theory (Van Evera 1997, 27-28). It is also "essentially an investigative process" (Miles and Huberman 1984, 37). Through the review of documents and interviews with participants in the Haiti response, this dissertation case will investigate the impact of paramilitary professional culture on the SOUTHCOM, FEMA, and the U.S. Coast Guard in recognizing, responding, organizing, and acting in the wake of the 2010 earthquake.

Sources for Research and Data

To attempt to answer how paramilitarism, career ladders, and workforce autonomy influence a DRO's speed into action, three primary sources have been drawn upon for research and data collection. First, literatures on organizations, culture, and disaster management (including the Haiti crisis) were studied for background information and research. These literatures frame the area for research and provide the scholarly nexus within which this work seeks to contribute.

Second, information was drawn from after action reports and other data sources that relate to the 2010 Haiti earthquake. For example, FEMA's after action report details the involvement of its incident management assistance teams (IMAT) and urban search and rescue teams (US&R) in the earthquake's aftermath (Lofton 2010). Other sources included the U.S. military's after action reports from the Haiti response, including lessons learned from General Ken Keen, the SOUTHCOM deputy commander who led JTF-Haiti; the lessons from the U.N. Office for the Coordinator of Humanitarian Affairs; and USAID's own after action reports (Keen 2010, Bhattacharjee and Lossio 2011, Guha-Sapir et al 2011). Organizational doctrine was examined for its influence on response operations, as well. Additional documents were drawn from the U.S. Coast Guard, SOUTHCOM, FEMA, the Red Cross, and other sources such as the GAO and Congressional Research Service. No documents described a holistic response to the Haiti earthquake; instead, they each focused on specific aspects of the response (i.e., U.N. perspective as described by Bhattacharjee and Lossio, or the DoD perspective as described by Keen et al); this paper may be the first towards a broader description of those events from different organizations' perspectives (Bhattacharjee and Lossio 2011, Keen et al 2010).

Third, semi-structured interviews were conducted with members of each organization, reflecting both organizational leadership (who presumably shape culture) and mid-level management personnel who were involved in specific aspects of the Haiti response (and who must operate with their agency cultures). A total of 19 interviews took place with senior government officials and members of each DRO involved in the Haiti response for this study. Interviews took place in Washington, DC, via video teleconference, or via telephone, and ranged in length from 45 minutes to two hours. Where agreed upon, audio recordings were made of the interviews for later reference, and recordings securely stored per university regulations in accordance with Institutional Review Board guidance.[7]

---

[7] Virginia Tech IRB approval was obtained in August 2013 for this research. IRB paperwork is on file in the University records.

II. RESEARCH DESIGN

Qualitative Case Study & Process Tracing

This dissertation employs a case study methodology, drawing data from aforementioned literatures, after action reports, and narratives from the Haitian earthquake, and the select interviews from DRO leaders. Case studies are an accepted method of qualitative inquiry, as described by Van Evera, Strauss et al, and Yin (Van Evera 1997, Strauss and Corbin 1998, Yin 2003). It is especially accepted in disaster research, as described by Stallings: some of the foundational disaster management scholarship is based upon numerous case studies. For example, early disaster research was performed by Quarantelli, Dynes, Haas, and others at the Disaster Research Center, and by Kreps (Stallings 2002). Quarantelli's "Inventory of Disaster Field Studies in the Social and Behavioral Sciences 1919 – 1979" details many of these research efforts (Quarantelli 1982). In using the case study methodology, this dissertation follows in the tradition of the Disaster Research Center studies. Organizational studies based on specific disasters have also been done by Wamsley and the National Academy of Public Administration (looking at Hurricane Andrew), and by Sylves (Wamsley 1996, Wamsley 1997, Sylves 1994).

Qualitative data analysis can be especially useful for investigating causal relationships in complex social settings. As stated by Miles and Huberman, "with qualitative data, one can preserve chronological flow, assess local causality, and derive fruitful explanations" (Miles and Huberman 1984, 1).

This research effort uses a technique known as process tracing to track the key actions and decisions made by the organizations and individuals as they began to recognize, respond, organize, and take action after the earthquake. As described both in Van Evera and Collier, process tracing is a descriptive process that "focuses on the unfolding of events or situations over time" (Collier 2011, 824). Van Evera describes it as the exploration of...

> ...the chain of events by which the initial case conditions are translated into case outcomes. The cause-effect link that connects independent variable and outcome is unwrapped and divided into smaller steps; then the investigator looks for observable evidence of each step (Van Evera 1997, 64).

In this case, the exploration of the influence of the larger aspect of paramilitary culture on each disaster response organization will be examined by looking at the differences in processes and events that related to workplace autonomy, career ladders, and paramilitarism. The process tracing technique is applied to the story of the three disaster response organizations, seeking to understand the decisions and challenges faced in the recognition, response, organization, and activity phases in the immediate aftermath of the earthquake. The effort attempts to link these independent variables to organizational action, to see whether they might have sped up or slowed down the ability to recognize, respond, organize, and act in the wake of the Haiti catastrophe. Logical sources for corroboration of observations are "people with whom one has talked and observed" (Miles and Huberman 1984, 37). The interviewees share their stories and thoughts, corroborating or discounting observations contained in the research framework based upon the dependent and independent variables.

Through the stories of the interviewees and research into the various government documents, after action reports, and incident narratives, this dissertation endeavors to provide some understanding of the degree to which these cultural variables helped or hindered the speed of these organizations in their initial response. Additionally, it may provide insight into how these variables influenced the individual decision-makers in each DRO during the initial days of the Haiti earthquake response effort.

This research was undertaken with the postulation that DROs are influenced in important ways by the variations in their paramilitary cultures, most importantly the speed at which they can recognize, respond, organize, and act in the face of a non-routine crisis. In this case, speed is more than just a time factor, but the ability to effectively and efficiently cycle through these four key phases, each leading towards positively "changing the outcome" for the disaster survivors.[8]

LIMITATIONS

The international and crisis aspects of the Haiti earthquake make it a laboratory for examining the influence of paramilitary cultural attributes on DROs; nevertheless, some potential challenges and limitations may be imposed by the selection of this case. Available information for some DROs may be limited, or a specific organization may not have played a very important role.

The memories, stories, and perspectives of the interviewees are inherently their own, with any personal bias "baked" into their narratives. This is inherent to qualitative analysis. Undoubtedly, this research can only scratch the surface. Hopefully, selecting experienced personnel who have worked in multiple disasters in many organizations over their careers has mitigated this limitation. The fact that the 19 interviewees represent over 500 years of cumulative experience in DROs holds promise that the findings are valid.

---

[8] A senior FEMA official described the President and the FEMA Administrator both agreeing on this phrase ("change the outcome") to describe the goal of the U.S. government's intervention during the first Cabinet meeting on Haiti after the earthquake. Interview with a senior FEMA official, December 20, 2013. Appendix A has a list of interviewees.

THIS PAGE INTENTIONALLY BLANK

CHAPTER III. LITERATURES: WHAT WE KNOW ABOUT PARAMILITARY CULTURE & DISASTER RESPONSE ORGANIZATONS

Organizational culture has been widely studied in public administration research, and seminal ethnographic studies like *The Forest Ranger* described the effects of organization culture long before James Q. Wilson broke down the institutional forces that shaped those organizational behaviors in *Bureaucracy* (Kaufman 1960, Wilson 1989). Aspects of military culture have been a studied subtopic within the area of organization culture, but paramilitary cultures, less so (for example, Huntington's work on the professionalization of the U.S. Army between the Civil War and World War I) (Huntington 1957).

This section discusses where this work fits in scholarship by describing what we know about disaster management, paramilitarism, career ladders, workforce autonomy, and the disaster response organizations observed in this paper. It starts with an overview of disaster literature, focusing on the conflicting paradigms of command and coordination, prior efforts to distinguish between different response organization types, differences between routine emergencies and crises, and differences between international and domestic disaster responses.

Disaster and emergency management has been a subject of special attention in public administration scholarship, starting back as early as 1941; in 1985 a special edition of *Public Administration Review* was devoted to emergency management and public administration, and other studies were done after focusing events like Hurricane Andrew and Hurricane Katrina (McReynolds 1941, Petak et al 1985, Odeen et al 1993, NAPA 2009). These were wide-ranging studies focusing on many facets of the disaster response challenge, from policy and politics to administrative design and organizational issues. As the field of emergency management has grown and attempted to professionalize, it has developed its own journals, associations, and professional conferences.

In the research on disasters, there is limited space devoted to the organization and culture of disaster response organizations, aside from a discussion of the general nature of centralized versus decentralized national policy towards disaster response, the command versus coordination paradigm, and international comparisons of the several nations' disaster response systems (Rodriguez 2007, 349-351). However, in the past decade there has been renewed emphasis on how to design and measure successful response to emergencies. This can be attributed to the aftermath of both the 9/11 attacks and Hurricane Katrina, and a myriad of other disasters that have occurred within the U.S. and abroad (including Haiti's earthquake, the Pacific Rim tsunami, the B.P. Deepwater Horizon accident, and the Fukushima nuclear catastrophe). For example, Roberts, Wamsley, and Ward describe the development of humanitarian aid via the Red Cross in the early 20th century, the emergence of civil defense approaches in response to the Cold War, and the establishment of the "all-hazards" approach to disaster management marked by the term of James Lee Witt as FEMA Administrator in President Bill Clinton's cabinet (Rubin 2012).

In the aftermath of Hurricane Katrina in 2006, the National Research Council reviewed much of the work in the disaster research field (Anderson 2006). Their report indicated that much of the research on disaster response and recovery was focused on hazards and hazard vulnerability, societal vulnerabilities and resilience, and sustainability (Anderson 2006, 124). Research in the response phase of disasters did include an emphasis on "situational assessment, crisis communication, coordination, and response management"

(Anderson 2006, 125). Much of the literature focused on the development of emergent inter-organizational networks. There has also been research into response failures, including the "failure to recognize the magnitude and seriousness of an event" (Anderson 2006, 141).

It is during this response phase when attention often focuses on individual organizations: FEMA has been a special target; Wamsley and others have given extensive treatment to FEMA and the National Guard in the times between Hurricane Andrew and the aftermath of Hurricane Katrina (Wamsley 1993, Wamsley 1997). There has also been limited work discussing the Red Cross and FEMA during Andrew and during the Loma Prieta earthquake (Carley and Harrald 1997, Neal 1992, Neal and Phillips 1997). More recently, Hamner took up an analysis of the transformation of the Red Cross Disaster Services' human resource system after Hurricane Katrina (Hamner 2008).

Two Incident Management Paradigms: Command and Control vs. Coordination

In disaster management literature, two management paradigms have dominated the discourse for building emergency response systems: the paradigm of "command and control" and the paradigm of "coordination" (mentioned in the literature first as the "problem-solving" model) occupy much of the scholarly discussions on disaster organizations and disaster response (Anderson 2006, 141-142). These models were heavily researched in the 1990s, with the "command and control" model being equated to a military, top-down, centralized control model, and the "coordination" model with networks, decentralization, and collaboration. Disaster management scholars such as Kreps, Waugh, and Sylves have discussed this topic, and the coordination model has been generally favored by both scholars and civilian emergency management practitioners (Kreps 1982, Kreps 1989, Waugh 2006, Sylves 2009). This has notably coincided with the emergence of the emergency management profession since the 1970s, as an evolution of the old civil defense model in the U.S., which was heavily focused on military hazards from the Cold War and whose practitioners were often retired military personnel (Rubin 2012). However, the U.S. has continued to rely heavily on military organizations for both domestic and international disaster relief, and the military has maintained its own scholarship on humanitarian assistance and disaster response (HA/DR) (Nagl and Young 2000).

Some have tried to navigate between the two paradigms of "command and control" and "coordination." Kettl and Allen have both described this as a key challenge for public administration (Kettl 2003, Allen 2012). Comfort's work in conducting a case study comparison of 11 earthquake responses revealed that an effective response depended upon an organizational ability to simultaneously sustain operating structures but also be flexible while handling rapidly changing disaster demands (Comfort 1999). Her focus was mainly on systems-level comparison, not on individual organizations, per se.

Despite the preference for the "coordination" model, the U.S. domestic system heavily relies on military-style command and control doctrine, for example in the National Incident Management System (NIMS), which focuses heavily on the concept of a scalable and flexible -- yet inherently unitary -- chain of command (FEMA 2008). The "command and control" paradigm remains present in practice.

Typologies of Disaster Response Organizations

Traditional public administration scholarship supported the mechanistic organizational form as a method of improving the efficiency and effectiveness of work: an organization has set characteristics (Weber 1946), an organization has division and coordination of work (Gulick 1937), an organization has informal and formal social norms

(Barnard 1938), and different situations often dictate different ways people give and take orders (Follett 1926). An essential element of public administration scholarship seeks to understand how organizational coordination is accomplished (Wilson 1989). Therefore, all disaster response agencies, as organizations, will have variations of these elements, and it may be worth understanding their variances, given the significance of disasters and their impact on society.

There have been several scholarly attempts at developing a typology to describe disaster response organizations. One of the first of these typologies was created by the Disaster Research Center (DRC, first at Ohio State University, now at the University of Delaware) ascribing behavioral characteristics to four different organizational responses to emergencies. Figure 3 illustrates this typology (Rodriguez 2007, 298).

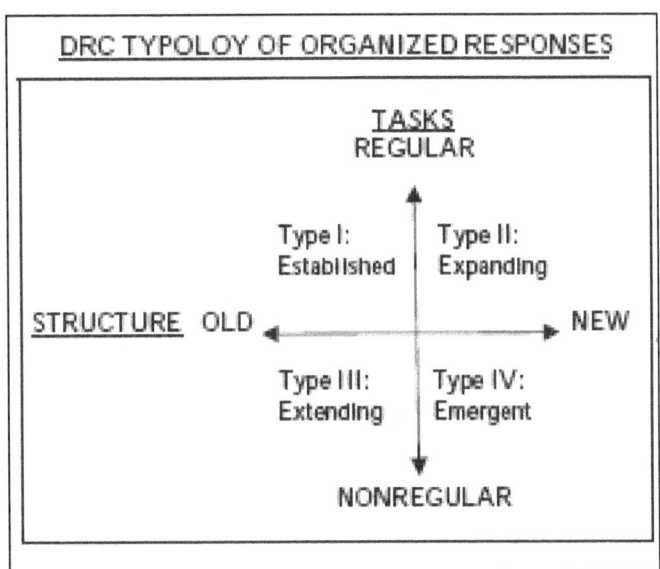

Figure 3. DRC TYPOLOGY OF ORGANIZED RESPONSES (Rodriguez 2007, 298).

The DRC typology describes organizational characteristics during a disaster along two axes: *tasks* and *structure*. Structures are described as either *old* or *new*, tasks are either *regular* or *non-regular*. This matrix results in four response types. In Type I (*established*) responses, the response organization existed before and event and does routine work within pre-established missions; in Type II (*expanding*) responses, the response organization pre-exists the crisis, but expands into new structural forms for a specific incident; Type III (*extending*) organizations pre-exist but play unique or novel roles in a disaster, such as undertaking an unforeseen mission; and Type IV (*emergent*) responses are almost entirely ad hoc for a given disaster, requiring novel organizational forms and novel missions (Rodriguez 2007, 298-300).

Another taxonomy of disaster organizations has been proposed by disaster studies scholar John Harrald, running along two axes of *agility* and *discipline* (see figure 4; Harrald 2006). Agility describes the organization's culture, as either *creative* or *rigid*. Discipline describes the organization's processes, as either *unstructured/undefined* or *well-structured/defined*. This typology yields four types of disaster response organizations: Type I (*dysfunctional*), Type II (*ad hoc/reactive*), Type III (*balanced/adaptive*), and Type IV (*bureaucratic/procedural*). Harrald proposes that the most effective DROs have a Type III (*balanced/adaptive*) culture, and he cites the U.S. Coast Guard as an exemplar of this Type III typology.

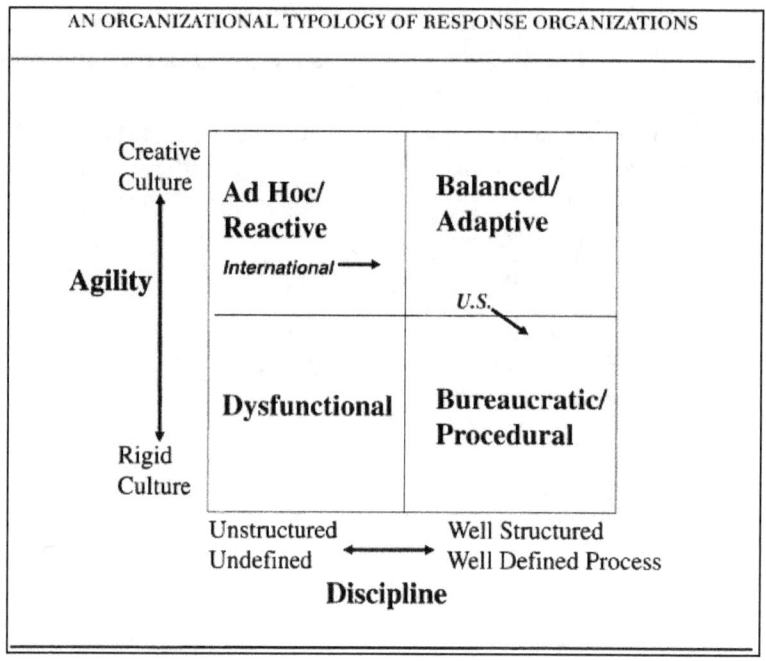

Figure 4. HARRALD'S TYPOLOGY OF DISASTER RESPONSE ORGANIZATIONS (Harrald 2006).

Both the DRC and Harrald typologies focus on the ways in which disaster organizations tend to behave in a crisis; this research paper seeks to dive more deeply into understanding how paramilitary culture influences those organizational behaviors, especially as the relate to speed. These two typologies therefore provide a mechanism to analyze the response of various DROs during the Haitian earthquake in 2010. This will be further explored for each of the observed DROs.

Different Types of Disasters: from Routine to Crisis

As forecast in the 2006 National Research Council report, after Hurricane Katrina the research on how to build effective response systems expanded (Anderson 2006). The work of Harvard's National Preparedness Leadership Initiative, for example, has focused heavily on the characteristics of successful response leaders, developing the concept of "meta-leadership" that is being widely taught to political and administrative leadership (Marcus, Dorn and Henderson 2006). Meta-leadership postulates that successful response leaders -- think of Admiral Thad Allen during Hurricane Katrina or B.P. Deepwater Horizon -- are able to lead up to political masters, across organizational and network silos to others, and down to subordinates in a way that creates a "unity of effort" among diverse response partners (Marcus et al 2007). In short, it describes a set of individual characteristics that help lead successfully within the "coordination" paradigm.

Others have researched the interaction between the organization and its task environment. Disaster researchers Dutch Leonard and Arnold Howitt, for example, have focused on the type of catastrophes that organizations face, distinguishing between two different types of emergencies: *routine* emergencies and *crisis* emergencies (Leonard and

Howitt 2007). According to Leonard and Howitt, routine emergencies present consistent problem sets that responders are trained and experienced to face: for example, firefighters responding to a house fire. Crisis emergencies present non-routine problem sets that responders are not trained nor experienced with handling on a routine basis.

Routine emergencies require a specific set of leadership skills among responders: *high awareness* of the nature of the situation; *comprehensive scripts* of step-by-step roles to deal with the emergency; *modest customization* of adapting general routines to the specific incidents; *precision execution* of the routine to deal with the incident; well-defined and *highly developed skills* learned through training; *leaders who are trained* in the situation and how to respond, practiced at organizing and directing the response, and selected based upon their past experiences; an *authority-based command presence*; use of *recognition-primed decision making* to determine the best course of action; and the creation of a *hierarchical organization* in the response structure.[9]

Crisis emergencies are different than routine emergencies. In contrast to routine emergencies, the novelty and complexity of crisis emergencies are characterized by *low awareness* of the entirety of the evolving event; a *lack of comprehensive scripts* or playbooks as to effective courses of action; the need to customize or *improvise responses* to suit the specific event; *tolerance of fault* in response efforts that would otherwise not be acceptable; *incompletely specified skills* to bring to the problem; a muted, more *collaborative command* presence, at least until a specific course of action is determined; *cognitive-driven decisions* through traditional analytic processes to determine the best course of action; and a *flattened organizational structure* at the beginning of the incident while information is being collected and shared. Table 3 illustrates the differences in these models. Routine emergencies would seem to lend themselves to the command and control response paradigm, with established organizations performing routine functions (DRC's established/type I and Harrald's bureaucratic/procedural response archetype); crisis emergencies would seem to require novel responses (DRC's emergent/type IV and Harrald's ad hoc/reactive response archetype). As we will discover, Haiti was a crisis, not just another emergency.

---

[9] Recognition-primed decision making (RPDM) models were developed by psychology researcher Gary Klein to determine how decisions were made under time constrained, stressful conditions, focusing on military officers and emergency workers. The RPDM research found that under emergent conditions like combat or an emergency, people quickly match the problem to a previously experienced solution that most closely resembles the situation, in lieu of thinking through progressive cognitive analyses. The analogy most used is that under these conditions, an individual's brain functions like a slide tray in an old projector, matching the closest slide to the situation for action (Klein 1996). The work can be seen as complementary with much of Karl Weick's sensemaking findings, such as in the Mann Gulch fire, where firefighters did not identify that their situation was non-routine quickly enough to survive (Weick 1993).

Routine vs. Crisis Emergencies	
ROUTINE	CRISIS
• High awareness • Comprehensive scripts • Modest customization • Precision execution • Highly developed skills • Trained leaders • Authority based command • Recognition primed decisions • Hierarchical organization	• Low awareness • Lack of scripts • Improvised response • Tolerance of fault • Incomplete skills • Collaborative command • Cognitive driven decisions • Flat organizations

Table 3. ROUTINE VS. CRISIS EMERGENCIES (Leonard and Howitt 2007).

Given a means of typing disaster organizations and a characterization of non-routine crisis events, we can begin to conceptualize a framework for comparing FEMA, the U.S. military, and the U.S. Coast Guard in the international response effort in Haiti.

Differences Between International and Domestic Response

The U.S. domestic and the international disaster response systems differ.[10] The domestic disaster response system in the United States has been described as a bottom-up system in which state and local governments have primacy for leading responses to disasters (with few exceptions, to include terrorist events where the Federal Bureau of Investigation (FBI) is designated as the lead agency). The federal government provides support to the state and local governments when a disaster occurs, coordinated by the Federal Emergency Management Agency (FEMA) under provisions of the Robert T. Stafford disaster relief act (FEMA 2012). The domestic system for response has been re-engineered and tweaked three times in the past decade (as FEMA rewrote the *National Response Plan* (2005), the *National Response Framework* (2006) and the new *National Response Framework* (2013)); nevertheless, it remains essentially a system in which responsibility for command, control, and coordination is directed by the state and local governments that are affected by the crisis. The U.S. domestic system employs the incident command system (ICS) hierarchical framework for coordinating disaster response. This system is described as the National Incident Management System, or NIMS (FEMA 2008).

The international system for disaster response differs from the U.S. system, since sovereign nations retain ultimate primacy over any aid that they receive from other nations. Delivery of international aid from around the globe is coordinated by several United Nations' offices, including the U.N. Office for Coordination of Humanitarian Affairs (OCHA), the World Food Program (WFP), and the World Health Organization (WHO).

The U.N. typically coordinates these efforts through a "cluster" system, which differs from the American ICS because there is no centralized command and control

---

[10]Richard Sylves provides a brief overview of these domestic and international systems (Sylves 2009).

hierarchy (UN 2013). The clusters are arranged around various humanitarian needs, such as nutrition, health, water/sanitation, emergency shelter, camp coordination/management, protection, early recovery, logistics, and emergency telecommunications. They could be considered analogous to the U.S. emergency support functions (ESF) within the U.S. National Response Framework; however, the U.N. clusters are more designed for long-term, unfolding humanitarian events (like famines or displacement of refugees) than for immediate crisis response. General Keen, the deputy commander of SOUTHCOM stated that the U.N. cluster system, "was not designed to respond to a disaster like this" (Luu 2013).

The clusters are intended to ensure representation of all stakeholders, with the U.N. acting as a "provider of last resort" (UN 2013). Coordination within each cluster derives from consensus and cooperation, with final approval of the host nation before action is taken. One member of the Red Cross described the cluster system as a "marketplace" where humanitarian organizations gather and exchange or bid on opportunities to provide aid in an ad hoc fashion; for example, a camp might need food for 1,000 people: several NGOs might negotiate who would handle that assignment.[11] From a public administration standpoint, it could be stated that the U.N. cluster system is designed to reflect the value of equity among response partners, whereas the U.S. ICS reflects the value of efficiency among those partners.

A variety of international nongovernmental organizations (NGOs) also provide disaster aid, for example, the International Red Cross. Figure 5 illustrates the complicated international relationships when a disaster occurs from the U.N. perspective, as described by a U.N. investigator for the Haiti earthquake crisis (Olafsson 2010).

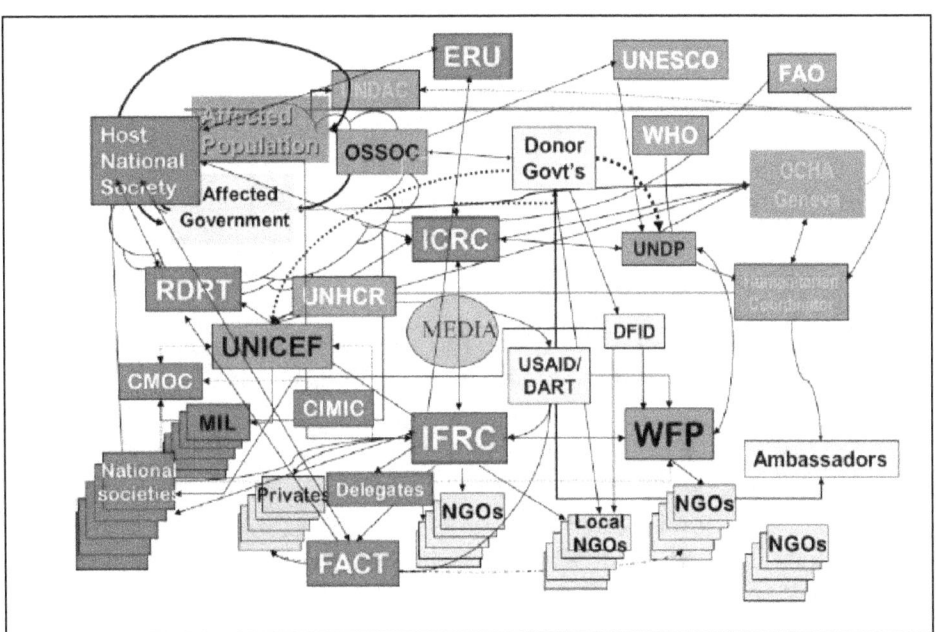

Figure 5. INTERNATIONAL DISASTER RESPONSE COORDINATION (Olafsson 2010).

The U.S. mechanism for assisting in international disasters in coordination with these organizations generally involves the Office of Foreign Disaster Assistance (OFDA) within the United States Agency for International Development (USAID), the State Department,

---

[11] Interview with a senior Red Cross official, American Red Cross, October 2013.

and the Department of Defense (through whichever military "combat command" has responsibility for the area of the disaster).[12] Combat commands are the Department of Defense's geographic division of its forces around the globe (Haiti falls under Southern Command's (SOUTHCOM) area of responsibility). FEMA, the main domestic U.S. federal disaster coordination agency, has not historically been involved in foreign disasters. Of note, the head of USAID, Dr. Rajiv Shah (a medical doctor with a background in global health issues), had been sworn into office only days before the earthquake (USAID 2010).

The U.S. ambassador in a foreign nation has the ultimate responsibility to declare a disaster and open up mechanisms for providing U.S. disaster relief (this is, in some ways, analogous to the role played by U.S. governors, with the caveat that the ambassador is not in charge of the host country's response like a governor in a U.S. state). America uses this procedure to respond regularly to international events; noteworthy among them have been the recent Pacific Rim tsunami in 2004 and Japan's earthquake, tsunami, and nuclear accident in 2011.

PARAMILITARISM AND MILITARY CULTURE

Culture underlies organizational life, and can be reflected in many aspects of agencies, such as symbols, ceremonies, rituals, and rights-of-passage; these can be referred to as artifacts of the culture (Trice and Beyer 1993). These cultural artifacts serve to bind a group together as a mechanism against external influence in the performance of the group's work (Schein 2004). Cultures that are strongly bound together can be viewed as "thick cultures"; they are also often heavily laden with artifacts (Cheng 1998, Wilson 2007).

The military has its own unique culture; the distinction of the military as a professional class with a distinct culture apart from the rest of society can be traced back to the time of the Roman legions. The modern American military and its culture are modeled after European allies, notably the Prussian and British militaries in the latter half of the 19th century (Huntington 1957, Coffman 2004).

While the first half of the American military experience (from the Revolution through the Civil War) consisted mainly of citizen-soldier militias and a gentlemen class that made up the officer ranks, the post-Civil War through World War I era saw the development of distinct professional military culture, consisting of full-time soldiers and officers who received professional training and education in officer schools like West Point and the Army War College. Military experience was gained through expeditionary deployments like the expansion into the Philippines at the turn of the 19th century (Huntington 1957).

The military also developed as an institution in politics and society, segregating and protecting the officer class (Rosen 1995). During this latter period, the military "made the great step forward of substituting a professional for a technical orientation at the service academies," as part of the development of this professional culture (Huntington 1957, 239). The modern American military has become a strongly-bound, thick culture, reflected in its uniforms, rank, insignia, and ceremony. Wamsley discussed this military culture in the early

---

[12]USAID, formerly an independent agency, was established in 1961 by President John F. Kennedy. Over the past decade it has been incrementally integrated into the Department of State through a series of budgetary and policy directives.

1970s, writing "the military is a subculture distinguishable from the larger general culture," and further:

> The fundamental values of the military subculture are: (1) acceptance of all-pervasive hierarchy and deference patterns; (2) extreme emphasis on dress, bearing, and grooming; (3) specialized vocabulary; (4) emphasis on honor, integrity, and professional responsibility; (5) emphasis on brotherhood; (6) fighter spirit marked by aggressive enthusiasm; (7) special reverence for history and traditions; (8) social proximity for dependents (Wamsley 1972, 401).

Military cultures are both built upon and reflective of doctrine. Doctrine can essentially be viewed as an organization's written description of the operational culture it is trying to create; it can also be viewed as the principles of performance for an organization or institution. A Navy captain described it as, "what we believe is the best way to do things, based on experience and knowledge."[13] For example, the USCG's capstone doctrinal publications states that doctrine consists of:

> ...fundamental concepts that guide our actions in support of the Nation's objectives. Rooted in our history and distilled of hard won experience, they provide a shared interpretation of that experience. This, in turn, provides a common starting point for thinking about future directions. Together with training and experience, this shared outlook leads to consistent behavior, mutual confidence, and more effective collective action without constraining initiative (USCG 2009, 2).

There are also subsets of military culture. For example, paramilitary cultures reflect a series of organizational characteristics that include aspects of military culture, but are not designed for the sole purpose of violence (Langston 2000). Organizations with paramilitary cultures could share a range of these attributes, such as hierarchy and centralized command, the use of symbols such as uniforms, insignia, and rank, ceremonies and rituals (e.g., saluting, or ceremonies like "changing of commands"), education that includes indoctrination for all new employees, and a cadre of leaders set apart by experience, education, and professional development. Research since the 1970s on paramilitary cultures have tended to focus on the impact of the militarization of domestic law enforcement agencies (for example, the expanding use of SWAT teams in domestic law enforcement agencies) or on the development of special police paramilitary commando units in developing nations (Kraska 1996, Kraska 1997, Chappel and Lanza-Kaduce 2010).

Many disaster response organizations reflect some of these military-like cultural facets (FEMA's Urban Search and Rescue teams are uniformed and hierarchical, for example); however, some research indicates that there are unique challenges when conducting disaster relief operations with a military force. This issue has been a problem for U.S. military forces in the past, which has not had a good history of managing the shift from security to disaster relief. Dr. John Nagl, a military scholar later noted for his work in writing on counterinsurgency doctrine during the Iraq conflict, wrote earlier in his career on the challenges of switching from a war-fighting posture to relief operations; noting, for

---

[13] Author's interview with a retired military officer, 2014.

example, that during Operation Restore Hope in Somalia, the U.S. Army units were "bewildered" by the overlap between warfighting and peacekeeping missions (Nagl and Young 2000).

This problem was perhaps most exemplified in the famous video images of General Russell Honoré imploring members of the 82nd Airborne Division to put away their rifles as they drove into downtown New Orleans after Hurricane Katrina (DeBerry 2010). As one lessons-learned report regarding Haiti's earthquake stated, the U.S. military is often the first to an affected region after a disasters; however:

> ...unlike conventional military operations, [commanders] often receive little or no warning before executing HA/DR operations. HA/DR operations also differ from conventional operations because the military frequently acts in a supporting role for partner nations, OGAs, NGOs, and IGOs. It is, therefore, essential for military personnel to effectively communicate and seamlessly coordinate efforts to the supported nations, its leaders, and affiliated agencies (Koch 2011).[14]

In other words, for HA/DR operations, which are often non-routine crisis events as opposed to routine military emergencies, the military needs to understand how to coordinate outside of a command and control framework that it uses during war.

WORKFORCE AUTONOMY: THE PROFESSIONS AND CULTURE

Organizational cultures can also be characterized by the types of professional attributes they exhibit. One of the prominent scholars on professions was sociologist Eliot Freidson, whose work focused heavily on the medical and legal fields. Over his career, Freidson established and evolved a framework for different work cultures, delincating between professions and the work done in the Weberian rational-legal bureaucracy, which Freidson also referred to as "managerialism" or the "firm" (Freidson 1986). As his theories evolved, he also distinguished a third type of work culture, referred to interchangeably as a "craft", "market", or "consumerism" (Freidson 2001). In the Freidson taxonomy, institutional organizational cultures can be characterized into one of these three categories: professions, bureaucracies, and tradecrafts.

Professions (also referred to as "occupations") have distinct characteristics in that include restrictions on entry, education and a distinct body of knowledge, control over division of labor, and autonomy. Professional organizations also tend to be more flat than hierarchical. In a profession, the individual employs discretion and control over the performance of his/her work (Freidson 1986, Freidson 2001).

Bureaucracy ("managerialism") is characterized by traditional Weberian aspects of the firm, including formal rules, written description of duties, pyramid organizational structures, and clear lines of authority. In a bureaucracy, managers control the work through rules, regulations, and processes (Freidson 1986, Freidson 2001). *Tradecrafts* tend to be skill-based, market-driven work in which the majority of skills are acquired through on the job

---

[14]HA/DR stands for humanitarian assistance/disaster response; OGA stands for other governmental agencies; and IGO stands for intergovernmental organizations.

training. In a craft, the customer controls the work based upon the demand for goods or services (Freidson 2001).

These three frames provide a specific way of comparing the working culture and the associated autonomy people have as they work within DROs. A humanitarian organization like the Red Cross, for example, might behave like a tradecraft during disaster relief in supplying food and shelter (while its separate blood supply services might, nevertheless, behave like a profession, with many licensed nurses). The military or FEMA might behave in a bureaucratic fashion, waiting for orders to be issued before responding; the "old" FEMA certainly fit this category when it would wait for states to request a presidential disaster declaration in accordance with the Stafford Act before moving response assets (Rubin 2012). A captain of a Coast Guard cutter, however, may enjoy a large degree of professional autonomy, based on the longstanding tradition of the independence and authority of a ship's captain at sea, and the initial instructions of Alexander Hamilton to the original revenue cutter service in 1790:

> Hence, it will be necessary for you from time to time to ply along the coasts in the neighborhood of your station, and to traverse the different parts of the waters which it comprehends (USCG *Pub 1* 2009, 101).

Like Michael Lipsky's "street-level bureaucrats", Coast Guard officers have tremendous leeway and autonomy in decisions they make as sea-faring bureaucrats (Lipsky 2010).

CAREER LADDERS: INSIDERS OR OUTSIDERS?

Whether employees are hired into service at entry level, or at mid or senior levels, also differentiates organizations. The military, for example, hires all new personnel at the bottom of the organization, where they must go through a unified indoctrination course ("boot camp", as mentioned earlier) and then segregates between officers and enlisted personnel. All U.S. Coast Guard or U.S. Army personnel start at the bottom, and work their way up, completing a series of training certifications, educational courses, and assignments to build experience. The Commandant of the Coast Guard has always come from with the organization, what can be termed an "internal" career ladder. The same model applies for the rest of the uniformed U.S. military. On the other hand, civilian organizations like FEMA routinely hire staff at all levels from outside their organizations, to include senior leadership. Since its establishment in 1979, the FEMA administrator has *never* been an internally promoted careerist member of the organization, but always an external political appointment.[15] In humanitarian organizations like the Red Cross, the CEO is often selected by a board of directors, many times from outside the organization. This model defines an "external" career ladder.

Internal processes have been a hallmark of civil service organizations over the past century and a half (Tolbert and Zucker 1983). While there are many ways to look at the

---

[15] Former Miami-Dade County Fire Chief R. David Paulison had been the politically appointed head of the U.S. Fire Administration, a division within FEMA, when he replaced Mike Brown after Hurricane Katrina. I characterize his appointment as external, as well. The use of the word "external" is intended to capture a non-careerist appointment orientation, whether political, or private, such as the Red Cross.

insider vs. outsider issue, such as numbers and turnover of political appointees and their success (see some of the work of Dull et al), this research focuses on determining what model each DRO uses, and attempts to determine if that might have influenced the Haiti response (Dull et al 2012). For example, USAID's leader, Dr. Rajiv Shah, was an outsider, a new political appointee with a background in medical aid and development; he likely hadn't yet found his way to the office restroom when the earthquake occurred; on the other hand, Thad Allen was a career Coast Guard officer who had spent over three decades rising through the USCG ranks to Commandant.

DISASTER RESPONSE ORGANIZATIONS

Organizations play a key role in disaster response. As first described by the Disaster Research Center decades ago, those organizations behave differently in response to non-regular crisis emergencies: they might do some routine work in traditional structures, others might adapt or change missions, and some might develop ad hoc to meet the needs of the incident (Rodriguez 2007, 298). All types were present in Haiti in response to the earthquake. These organizations also possessed varying attributes of paramilitary culture. As has been discussed, disaster response literature has generally treated military command and control approaches to disaster response negatively, yet Harrald's research also suggests that organizations with a balanced and adaptive culture might be more effective in facing complex crises than other types of organizational cultures; ironically, the DROs with balanced and adaptive cultures seem to be ones that possess a higher degree of paramilitary culture (Harrald 2006). This section explores the organizational history and culture of the USCG, FEMA, and SOUTHCOM, laying a foundation that might give insight into how to reconcile this discrepancy, and perhaps illuminate ways to build better, faster disaster response organizations.

U.S. COAST GUARD

"It's just effective soup."[16]

One of the oldest disaster response organizations in America is the U.S. Coast Guard (USCG). It has a long history of responding to significant disasters, from flooding in the Midwestern United States in the 1880s, to the San Francisco earthquake of 1906, through modern-era disasters like 9/11 (2001), Hurricane Katrina (2005), and the Deepwater Horizon explosion and oil spill (2010) (USCG Disaster History 2013). The USCG was among the first American organizations to respond to the Haitian earthquake in 2010.

The USCG traces its roots to 1790, when George Washington commissioned the creation of a 10-ship fleet to enforce U.S. tariffs and combat smuggling; it was known then as the Revenue Cutter Service. It pre-dates the U.S. Navy by eight years (USCG History 2013). Since its establishment, it has merged with the U.S. Lifesaving Service, the U.S. Lighthouse Service, and the Bureau of Marine Inspection and Navigation, evolving into a multi-mission organization that handles a wide array of maritime responsibilities, from search and rescue, to environmental protection, to maritime regulation, navigation, and safety. It was transferred from the U.S. Department of Transportation into the newly established Department of Homeland Security in 2003.

The USCG conducts both homeland security and non-homeland security missions. Its homeland security missions include ports, waterways and coastal drug interdiction; migrant interdiction; defense readiness; and other law enforcement activities. Its non-homeland security missions include marine safety, search and rescue, aids to navigation, living marine resources, marine environmental protection, and ice operations (Richards 2011).

Unique to the USCG is its dual authority as a U.S. military force and as the chief maritime federal law enforcement agency, a combination of authorities not shared by other military forces or other federal law enforcement agencies. It is both military and paramilitary.

USCG Doctrine

The USCG promulgates its doctrine through a series of capstone documents. These documents begin with *Coast Guard Publication 1: The U.S. Coast Guard, America's Maritime Guardian*, known as *Pub 1* (USCG 2009). *Pub 1* provides an overview of the USCG roles and missions, force structure, history, ethos, and core values as a military, multi-mission, maritime service. Of note, it elucidates seven principles serve as directives for USCG officers and enlisted crews in their operational activities; these principles include:

- clear objective
- effective presence
- unity of effort
- on-scene initiative
- flexibility
- managed risk
- restraint.

---

[16] Author's phone interview with a Coast Guard officer, August 22, 2013.

The principle of *clear objective* states that "every operation should be directed towards a clearly defined and obtainable objective" (USCG 2009, 77)

The principle of *effective presence* states that assets and capabilities must be "in the right place at the right time" (USCG 2009, 78). It refers to the patrol characteristics of the service that go back to its initial founding "Letter of Instruction" from Alexander Hamilton.

The principle of *unity of effort* describes the need for the USCG to operate in partnership and transparency with other agencies. This principle also discusses the challenge of leading external agencies that are not under the USCG chain of command (USCG 2009, 81).

The principle of *on-scene initiative* states clearly that "Coast Guard men and women be given latitude to act quickly and decisively within the scope of their authority, without waiting for direction from higher levels in the chain of command. Personal initiative has always been crucial to the success of our Service" (USCG 2009, 82).

The principle of *flexibility* ascribes the ability of the USCG personnel to quickly shift between missions, for example, going from a maritime security patrol quickly into a search and rescue operation, as they shift between homeland security and non-homeland security missions.

The principle of *managed risk* describes the risk-based approach commanders should take to balancing capabilities and mission (USCG 2009, 86).

The principle of *restraint* describes the delicate balance between carrying out maritime military and law enforcement functions while maintaining restraint and prudence in their duties, reflecting its role in enforcing the laws of a free society (USCG 2009, 88). Like the principle of effective presence, this also is a reference to Alexander Hamilton's initial charge to the first revenue cutters.

These seven doctrinal principles describe the operational culture the USCG endeavors to reflect. The USCG doctrine provides a high degree of autonomy to its personnel.

Other documents also provide guidelines for disaster response. For example, the USCG has been one of the longest practicing agencies using the incident command system (ICS), and describes its use of the ICS in the USCG *Incident Management Handbook*. ICS is a scalable and flexible framework for coordinating response to all types of emergencies (USCG Incident Management Handbook 2006).

Career Ladders for USCG officers

The Coast Guard has a professional development system that provides a combination of training, education, and experience for its officers. This professional development program embeds the USCG aspirational doctrine into the knowledge, skills, and abilities within each USCG member and officer. Training consists of indoctrination and the learning of technical skills, both as basic learning and continued learning as the officer's career progresses. Formal education and leadership indoctrination occurs through a 17-week officer candidate school; additionally, many Coast Guard officers have gradated from either the USCG Academy or the Merchant Marine Academy, both top flight military colleges on equal standing with U.S. Naval Academy or the U.S. Military Academy (USCG Initial Training 2013). Officers' careers progress through a series of operational tours of duty, in command of ships in the cutter fleet or aircraft, and staff tours of duty in managerial, policy, or training roles.

The professional development for all USCG positions is linked together by a leadership guide that articulates 28 competencies. These competencies are grouped into four general leadership areas: leading self, leading others, leading performance and change, and leading the Coast Guard. Table 4 shows the 28 USCG leadership competencies.

Leading Self	Leading Others	Leading Performance & Change	Leading the Coast Guard
Accountability and responsibility	Effective communications	Conflict management	Financial management
Aligning values	Team building	Customer focus	Technology management
Followership	Influencing others	Decision-making and problem solving	Human resource management
Health & well-being	Mentoring Respect for others & diversity management	Management & process improvement	External awareness
Personal conduct		Vision development & implementation	Political savvy
Technical proficiency	Taking care of people		Partnering
		Creativity and innovation	Entrepreneurship
			Stewardship
			Strategic thinking

Table 4: USCG LEADERSHIP COMPETENCIES (USCG Leadership Development Framework 2006).

Additionally, the USCG offers specific, continuing education programs that deal with the development of the knowledge, skills, and abilities for disaster work. Four courses are listed in the USCG *International Training Handbook* for command "Operations Ashore." They include *Basic Preparedness and Exercise, Contingency Preparedness Planner, International Crisis Command and Control*, and *On-Scene Coordinator Crisis Management* (USCG 2008). Three additional crisis management courses are delivered that include *Maritime Crisis Management/Incident Command System 100/210/300, Emergency Operations Center*, and *Incident Response Planning (ICS 341)* (USCG 2008).

The training, education, and experience help create a flexible, agile, and adaptive culture. Leadership and autonomy is granted to USCG officers at a very early stage of their careers. Young officers, for example, are placed in charge of smaller USCG cutters (USCGC) very early on. They are likely to take command of a ship as a lieutenant, very early in their career, and then have several command and staff assignments in increasing responsibility.[17] Therefore, they learn operational leadership skills far ahead of other maritime peers. As a comparison, for example, a U.S. Navy officer is unlikely to have been placed in command of a ship until they reach the rank of Commander at approximately the 20-year mark in their Navy career. Autonomy provided to USCG officers also stems from its centuries-old seafaring tradition, where ships are given general orders to patrol a specific area and conduct a wide-variety of missions while "steaming" independently at sea.[18]

The USCG also has a long history of working with maritime partners to get things done. One USCG captain stated, "The Coast Guard is so small it can't get all it's tasked with done alone to achieve desired National outcomes. Therefore, we are very good at building

---

[17] Author's interview with senior USCG officer, 2013.
[18] While steam-powered ships have long since vanished from the fleet, this term is still used to describe the movement of ships on the ocean.

joint relationships."[19] Ports, for example, are supervised by the USCG, requiring collaboration and coordination with private port authorities, shipping companies, customs and law enforcement agencies, local boaters and fishermen, and the occasional local yacht club.

During disasters, the USCG often uses skills similar to those required to run a ship: the provision of electric power, food, safety, the launching and recovery of boats and aircraft, and surveys of the environment are done as part of routine missions, and are just scaled upwards during disaster operations.[20]

The USCG culture is autonomous, technically proficient, service oriented, capable, and fungible. In the words of the same officer, these ingredients are "just effective soup." This officer stated, however, that this culture was *not* the result of the doctrine or the procedures. He indicated that the official promulgation of doctrine was "reverse-engineered" over the past 10-15 years, to basically "describe what we were already doing."[21]

The USCG organization is imbued with characteristics that fit Harrald's balanced/adaptive (type III) disaster organization archetype. The doctrine and manuals describe a well-defined structure of USCG operations and the USCG principles clearly articulate a desired culture of flexibility and autonomy for officers in the performance of their duties.

Independent Variables	
Paramilitarism	Thick
Career Ladder	Insider
Workforce Autonomy	High

Table 5. USCG INDEPENDENT VARIABLES.

---

[19] Author's interview with a USCG officer, 2013.

[20] Ibid.

[21] Ibid. This was certainly a surprising and interesting point that calls for further study, in line with "which comes first, the chicken or the egg" (i.e., the doctrine or the culture)? It was nevertheless beyond the scope of this effort.

FEDERAL EMERGENCY MANAGEMENT AGENCY

"FEMA is the only organization where you issue the directive and then the debate begins."[22]

The Federal Emergency Management Agency (FEMA) was formed in 1979, a byproduct at the tail end of President Jimmy Carter's administration. Prior to the creation of FEMA, domestic emergency management and crisis response functions were spread across a hodgepodge of seven civilian and military government organizations (Farazmand 2001, 369). The agency's creation was an effort to consolidate many federal government programs related to both civil defense and disaster relief, many of which had been built up with the increasing role of the federal government in domestic disaster response that had evolved in the 20th Century (Farazmand 2001, 361; Rubin 2012). The consolidation of these federal functions occurred in the aftermath of the Three Mile Island nuclear power plant disaster, and was based on internal reviews from both the legislative and the executive branches (National Preparedness Task Force 2006, 18).

FEMA's creation consolidated the Federal Insurance Administration, the National Fire Prevention and Control Administration, the National Weather Service Community Preparedness Program, the Federal Preparedness Agency, and the Federal Disaster Assistance Administration. Civil defense activities were transferred to FEMA from the Department of Defense (National Preparedness Task Force 2006).

With the inauguration of Ronald Reagan in 1980, the agency was taken quickly in the direction of civil defense and national security, a combination of the President Reagan's focus on the Cold War struggle with the Soviet Union and the predilection of Reagan's choice for FEMA administrator, Louis Giuffrida, a general in the California National Guard and a civil defense adviser to the former governor, now president. Rather quickly, FEMA developed into a civil defense-focused organization, and Giuffrida's tenure was marked by political cronyism, a secretive organizational culture, and misuse of taxpayer funds. Giuffrida filled political positions with trusted friends, many former military police officers; many employees held Top Secret clearances and even carried sidearms, and numerous questionable expenditures took place, including the award of noncompetitive grants to groups where Giuffrida had been an adviser (Roberts 2013, 57-94). Under investigation by the Department of Justice and several Capitol Hill committees, Giuffrida resigned in 1985, but the culture and course of FEMA as a political backwater had been established, and its career ladder was imbued with an outsider orientation in the selection of personnel (Farazmand 2001, 373-377).

In the following years, a series of unremarkable directors held the post, and failures in responding to the 1989 Loma Prieta earthquake in California and the 1990 Hurricane Hugo led to some of the most notable historical quotes about its ineffectiveness, from Senator Ernest Hollings ([FEMA is] "the sorriest bunch of bureaucratic jackasses") to Congressman Norman Mineta ([FEMA] "could screw up a two car parade"), the agency could not shake its initial flaws and floundering operations (Farazmand 2001, 377-378).

The response to Hurricane Andrew in 1992 proved the final inauspicious act of this first version of FEMA. Within days of the landfall of the hurricane, facing the criticism of 200,000 homeless Florida citizens, and under the newly emergent glare of CNN cameras and the developing 24-hour news cycle, President George H.W. Bush dispatched 20,000 troops and sent his Secretary of Transportation, Andrew Card, to assume leadership of federal

---

[22] Author's interview with a senior FEMA official, 2013.

efforts, bypassing the existing FEMA structures that had been put in place (Wamsley 1996). It was an early historical prequel to the actions of President George W. Bush and FEMA during Hurricane Katrina in 2005; ironically, the chief of staff during Katrina for George W. Bush was the very same Andrew Card.

Many scholars have documented the renaissance FEMA underwent with the leadership of James Lee Witt during the Clinton presidency, including Wamsley, Farazmand, Khademian, Rubin, and Roberts (Wamsley 1996, Farazmand 2001, Khademian 2002, Roberts 2006, and Rubin 2012). Witt was the first administrator who had previous experience as an emergency manager, having served as Arkansas emergency management director during Bill Clinton's term as governor. Unlike Giuffrida, however, Witt had a personal relationship with the President. Under his leadership, he assured that The White House only sent to FEMA other political appointees with prior emergency management experience, restored merit promotions for career staff, reduced the footprint of the secret national security programs in the agency, and shifted the organization's focus and culture away from the Cold War civil defense posture towards the modern "all-hazards" approach to disasters that integrated response for natural disasters with its many national security continuity of government programs (Farazmand 2001, 404). The high water mark for FEMA was when President Clinton elevated Witt to a member of the President's cabinet in 1996 (Farazmand 2001, 410).

The FEMA cabinet position did not survive into the George W. Bush administration. Bush appointed Joe Allbaugh, his chief of staff as governor of Texas and presidential campaign director, to the administrator position (Lewis 2008). Although Allbaugh directed FEMA through the 9/11 attacks, FEMA's role in 9/11 was minimal; mainly it dispatched urban search and rescue teams to New York and the Pentagon, and provided disaster recovery grant funds (Roberts 2013). The majority of the scholarly and political aftermath of 9/11 focused on the "failure to connect the dots" and the holes in America's borders, security infrastructure, and intelligence (Keane 2002). Allbaugh resigned when FEMA was absorbed into the newly created Department of Homeland Security in 2003. He was replaced by his Deputy Director and former FEMA General Counsel, Mike Brown.

FEMA's performance under Brown during Hurricane Katrina mirrored many of the mistakes that occurred during Hurricane Andrew; but in this case the incident resulted in the deaths of between 1,200 and 1,800 Americans, and was combined with the embarrassing failure of the emergency management system subsumed under the newly formed homeland security apparatus (U.S. House of Representatives 2006, The White House 2006, Rubin 2012; Olsen 2010; Boin et al 2010, 707). After his "heck 'uv a job," Brown was stripped of leadership authority on September 9, 2005, about 10 days into the disaster, when Coast Guard Admiral Thad Allen assumed operational coordination of the federal response. Brown ultimately resigned and was replaced by U.S. Fire Administrator R. David Paulison, the former fire chief of Dade County, Florida.

Paulison's tenure was marked by an effort to renew FEMA, reestablishing the "lean forward" posture that Witt had started to impose to replace the past culture where FEMA would wait until a state asked for assistance. Paulison replaced numerous inexperienced political appointees and used a small cadre of advisors to begin to reshape the hobbled agency. Coast Guard Admiral Harvey Johnson became his deputy administrator and chief operating officer. The emergency management community took advantage of the policy window that opened up to attempt to re-establish prominence that many had felt the agency had lost in the consolidation into the Department of Homeland Security. In this wave,

Congress passed the Post Katrina Emergency Management Reform Act (PKEMRA), re-establishing the FEMA administrator as a direct report to the President during national emergencies, a role that had been subordinated to the Secretary of Homeland Security when DHS was established in 2003 (PKEMRA 2006).

Craig Fugate, the Florida state emergency manager under Governors Jeb Bush and Charlie Christ, was appointed by President Barack Obama to take over the reins at FEMA in 2009. After a quiet first two years, Fugate brought aggressive changes to FEMA, implementing a qualification system for FEMA operations staff, reinventing FEMA's part-time disaster assistance employees (DAEs) as a reservist program, and building off of the "all-hazards" approach to preparedness and the "whole of government" approach to problem solving with what he referred to as the "whole community" approach to emergency management.[23] The all-hazard approach treats hazards, whether natural (e.g. a tornado) or manmade (e.g. terrorism), in an inclusive fashion that requires similar preparedness, response, recovery, and mitigation efforts. It is a counterpoint the older, civil defense model, which had different, scenario-based mechanisms for preparedness for natural hazards and national security threats like nuclear war. Under the all-hazard approach, emergency management efforts take a general view that while each specific hazard or thereat might be different, the preparedness approaches are generally similar: determine the risk, prepare through training and exercises, and take action should an event occur (for example, evacuating to a safe location).

In an all-hazards model, emphasis is often placed on building capacity and *capabilities* for disaster response; in the civil defense model, hazards and threats are considered unique and different, requiring different hazard-specific *plans* to be created for each contingency. In the whole government model, inter-agency, inter-governmental approaches are taken to deal with emergent problems. The "whole of government" terminology was first used in the U.S. at the beginning of the Obama administration to describe a cross-agency approach to a variety of wicked policy problems. As the Obama administration began referring to "whole of government" approaches, in 2010 Craig Fugate built off that term and began to use the term "whole of community" (later shortened to "whole community") to describe his view on how the nation needed to respond to worst-case catastrophic emergencies, what he also termed the "maximum of maximum" scenario, or MoM (FEMA 2011).[24] The MoM scenario involved over 300,000 fatalities and 300,000 casualties based upon a no-notice (e.g. no advanced warning) emergency, such as a nuclear attack or the rupture of the New Madrid seismic fault in mid-west America. The scale of the disaster was eerily similar to Haiti's earthquake. Fugate believed that during such a large catastrophe, no level of government could handle the needs of survivors, so a community-wide response involving the private sector, faith groups, and individuals would be needed to fill in gaps. Empowering this inclusive thinking into FEMA's culture became his key effort, shaping its very doctrine for emergency response. Fugate established an aspirational performance metric that would combine the maximum of maximum planning scenarios with the whole community approach:

---

[23] Author's observations as a member of the Department of Homeland Security in the first six months of the Obama administration, and later working with FEMA as a member of the Homeland Security Studies and Analysis Institute during this time period.

[24] The author supported FEMA in an analytic role at this time and directly observed this shift in terminology.

Key benchmarks for FEMA's response and recovery resulting from a catastrophic event are to stabilize the event to meet the needs of survivors within 72 hours, restore basic services and community functionality within 60 days, and return communities to normalcy within five years (FEMA *State of FEMA* 2012).

FEMA Response Doctrine

FEMA has lacked doctrine for most of its history. Only recently was a formal doctrine established, promulgated through a FEMA document known as *Federal Emergency Management Agency Publication 1* (a mirror of the U.S. Coast Guard doctrinal process -- perhaps not a surprise due to the numerous former Coast Guard officers, including Deputy Administrator Harvey Johnson and current Assistant Administrator for Response Joe Nimmich, who became members of FEMA after Hurricane Katrina) (FEMA *Pub 1* 2010). However, most of FEMA's retired military personnel were more "order executors" than "order givers" in the military.[25]

The lack of a formal doctrine, however, didn't mean that there wasn't a set way of things getting done. In fact, based on its initial executive order establishing the agency, as well as authorizing legislation in the form of the Robert T. Stafford Disaster Relief Act, FEMA had a distinct way of operating within the U.S. federalism system from its beginning, up until James Lee Witt arrived in 1992. The key characteristic for FEMA operations in its early years was to wait for a request for a disaster declaration and request for help from a state governor before going into action. Hurricane Andrew's devastation of Southeastern Florida, and the subsequent problems with response, allowed Witt and his staff to begin to establish operations where items were pre-positioned prior to approaching disasters. During flooding in 1993, the changes were noticed, "This is the first time we have had this coordination in my experience," stated the Minnesota director of emergency management (Farazmand 2001, 393).

FEMA's merger into DHS and the early years of the George W. Bush administration likely stunted the further development of the organization, so that the failures during Hurricane Katrina seemed a complete regression back to the early approaches of waiting for the failure of governments in New Orleans and Baton Rouge (the state capital) before resources were moved. While Louisiana Governor Blanco was slow to call for aid, and then asked for "everything," many statements by FEMA administrator Mike Brown indicated that while he thought aid was moving, it had not:

> I think that one of the biggest mistakes that I made as the FEMA director during Katrina was not immediately turning to the military and saying: "We have been overwhelmed. We need you to take over logistics, distribution of commodities, etc." (Frontline 2005).

The system had broken completely.

Administrator David Paulison replaced Brown, picked up the broken pieces, and began to restore the advanced deployment of resources prior to a disaster declaration, including the establishment of "Pre-scripted Mission Assignments" with the Department of Defense. He began describing the "new FEMA" that would again have a "lean forward

---

[25] Author's interview with a senior FEMA official, 2013.

posture" in anticipation of the need of state and local governments.[26] His tenure was focused on this effort, which was essentially a rebuilding towards the James Lee Witt version of FEMA, but maintaining its integration within the Department of Homeland Security.[27]

Craig Fugate, President Obama's choice to lead FEMA, made this unofficial FEMA doctrine official, building upon the "lean forward" construct. Fugate summarized his philosophy as "go big, go early, go fast, be smart" (FEMA *State of FEMA* 2012). Fugate and his staff have overseen three significant changes in FEMA's response doctrine: the reformation of the workforce under the "FEMA Qualifications System," or FQS, the establishment of the aforementioned "whole community" philosophy of engaging non-traditional partners, and managing the implementation of The White House's *Presidential Policy Directive-8*'s overhaul of national preparedness (Obama 2011, FEMA 2011, Parkyn 2011). In 2010, FEMA released its first official doctrine product, *FEMA Publication 1*, intended to articulate its response philosophy (FEMA *Pub 1* 2010). Like the Coast Guard doctrine, it describes a set of ideal core values and guiding principles. However, unlike USCG doctrine, which is a description of the way the USCG has done business since 1790, the FEMA document is more aspirational, intended to describe the ideal state that the organization is striving to achieve. The core values described in *FEMA Publication 1* are compassion, fairness, integrity, and respect. Eight guiding principles are cited: teamwork, engagement, getting results, preparation, empowerment, flexibility, accountability, and stewardship (FEMA Pub 1 2010).

Despite these efforts, FEMA remains a managerially controlled structure that is heavily bureaucratic and confusing to stakeholders, with various silos between the organizations preparedness, mitigation, and operational programs, and a disjointed chain of command between its Washington headquarters its 10 FEMA regions, and its field units. These issues were brought to light during Hurricane Sandy, as conflict arose between decisions made at the FEMA regional office level, headquarters, and its Incident Management Assistant Teams in the Joint Field Office (JFO) (FEMA 2013).[28]

One Katrina survivor described continual frustration in dealing with FEMA's people and processes:

> Someone pointed out a young man about 40 feet
> away and said he was the "FEMA guy". I asked him if he was the "FEMA
> guy" and he said yes. I began to ask what was the procedure for filing a
> claim; did we need to be at our home site when the FEMA adjustor came by;
> how long before we could expect an adjustor; are FEMA benefits offset by

---

[26] Author's interview with a R. David Paulison, 2013.

[27] After Katrina, the controversy of whether FEMA should be in DHS or out was raised, with the emergency management community largely in favor of its independence, but many Bush administration and legislative leaders unconvinced that its wholesale independence was the right direction. Congress weighed options but the organization remained within DHS (Hogue and Bea 2006). This controversy remained until the decision by the Obama administration early in his Presidency to retain FEMA in DHS. This issue is perhaps only resolved for the moment; symbolically, the new FEMA headquarters building at the planned DHS headquarters campus on the old St. Elizabeth's hospital site had FEMA outside of the security perimeter and the other DHS agencies inside the perimeter. While statements were made that this design was done to intentionally avoid the security cordon because FEMA had many visitors, the author was privilege to some discussions with senior DHS officials that this was also a convenient way of hedging in the case that FEMA was ever separated from the Department. Author's personal observations, 2008.

[28] The author was part of a Hurricane Sandy review effort that involved site visits to the JFO in New Jersey, where numerous FEMA staff cited this conflict. Author's personal observations, 2012.

insurance payments, and so on. He said that he did not really know the answers but he would find out and if I came back, tomorrow he would have some answers for me. I noticed that he was wearing a dark blue T-shirt with the logo of a Volunteer Fire Department. I asked if he was a FEMA employee and he said he was not. He was a volunteer fireman from West Virginia. He was down in Mississippi trying to help. I asked him where the closest FEMA person was and he said he did not know. I asked if he was in charge of the parking lot. He said no. I said, "Now. Look around the parking lot and point out the highest ranking FEMA person here." He pointed to a guy at the far end of the lot and said, "I think it's the guy in the 'boonie' hat." We walked down to where he was. He had on a dark blue golf shirt with some undecipherable letters on the left breast. I asked if he was the FEMA guy. He said yes. I asked him a couple of questions and I started getting the same vague answers. When I asked if he was an actual FEMA employee he said no, that he was a volunteer fireman from Pittsburgh. He was just down trying to help. I asked him who his boss was and he did not know. I asked him what his job was and he said, "To pass out these brochures." He said that FEMA had put out a call for volunteer firemen to help supplement their employees. He volunteered, so they sent him to Mississippi. I asked him where the closest actual FEMA employee was, and he said he thinks it would be Atlanta. I thanked him for volunteering to help, but told him that I wanted to talk to FEMA. He said he understood and would try to get some answers by tomorrow. We gave up on FEMA for that day (Birdsall 2009, 522).

Many of FEMA's disaster responders were outsiders, operating without a clear chain of command, and with very low autonomy and limited ability to act on the needs of disaster survivors. Sylves, Wamsley, Lewis, and Roberts and have all discussed the high percentage of political appointees at FEMA (Sylves 1994, Wamsley 1996, Lewis 2008, Roberts 2013). Additionally, FEMA relies on many part time disaster responders (its former Disaster Assistance Employees, now rebranded as Disaster Reserve Corps) and contractors; in a 2012 study, Keelean found that, "the total steady-state workforce consists of 7,640 employees. The total response workforce -- that is the maximum number of personnel that FEMA could deploy if needed -- consists of 14,743 employees", indicating that almost half its disaster response force is brought from outside (Keelean 2012, 17-23).

FEMA does have many former military personnel, but it lacks a formal indoctrination program to build a shared perspective among all its employees. FEMA staffers have described its culture as fragmented, with civilian cultures in its legacy grant and preparedness programs and different cultures in its operational branches, and different cultures between headquarters, the regions, and its field teams.[29]

FEMA's urban search and rescue (US&R) teams bear the closest resemblance to a paramilitary unit. They are trained and equipped to rescue people from collapsed buildings, and their personal protective gear resembles military uniforms; however, they are made up of local government firefighters, paramedics, engineers, and physicians who are only activated by FEMA for emergencies. They are not full-time FEMA personnel.

---

[29] Author's interview with FEMA staff, 2013.

FEMA's Incident Management Assistance Teams (IMAT) also use a paramilitary-like hierarchy based on the incident command system to coordinate federal support to state and local governments in disasters, but FEMA's three national IMAT teams consist of approximately 25 personnel each, even though one government study found that FEMA has over 300 different designated incident management positions it is required to fill in a disaster (Parkyn 2011). Another study found that FEMA has only 912 staff specifically assigned to disaster response roles out of a workforce of 7,640; the remaining staff is assigned to various training, planning, grant-processing, and administrative roles (Keelean 2012, 18). FEMA has no formal ceremonies and inconsistent, if any, rights of passage. It remains an outsider-oriented culture, with thin levels of paramilitarism, and limited workforce autonomy.

Independent Variables	
Paramilitarism	Thin
Career Ladder	Outsider
Workforce Autonomy	Low

Table 6. FEMA INDEPENDENT VARIABLES.

SOUTHCOM/JTF-HAITI

"So often these days, the face of America is that of a soldier"[30]

U.S. Southern Command (SOUTHCOM) traces its roots to the end of World War II, when it was formed as the U.S. Caribbean Defense Command. Over several decades the area of responsibility (AOR) for the command shifted, from the Caribbean (which was reassigned to the Atlantic Command in Virginia) to Central and South America. During this time, it guarded the Panama Canal and developed training programs with Latin American military forces, and the command's headquarters was located in Panama. The Kennedy administration changed its name to Southern Command in 1964 reflecting its expanded AOR (SOUTHCOM 2014).

In the 1980s, under the policy directives of the Reagan administration, SOUTHCOM became involved with drug interdiction operations. In 1995, it regained the Caribbean AOR back in another Department of Defense realignment. With the implementation of the Panama Canal Treaties that called for the transfer of control of the canal back to Panama, SOUTHCOM's headquarters was relocated to Miami, Florida in 1997 (Rohter 1997). Figure 5 shows SOUTHCOM'S current AOR.

Figure 6. SOUTHCOM AOR (SOUTHCOM 2014).

Periodically, SOUTHCOM has been involved in regional humanitarian assistance and disaster response operations. When Hurricanes Georges and Mitch struck the Caribbean and Central American in 1998, SOUTHCOM mobilized over 20,000 troops to assist in relief operations (SOUTHCOM 2014).

---

[30] Martin 2010.

Today, SOUTHCOM maintains its AOR with four key missions: detainee operations, contingency response, countering transnational crime, and building partner capacity. Detainee operations include the support and maintenance of operations at Guantanamo Bay, Cuba for military prisoners from the Global War on Terror. Contingency response includes the readiness for military action with the AOR and in support of other commands around the world. Countering transnational crime focuses on interdicting the illicit flows of people and goods in the region, including drug and narcotics trafficking, money flows, and illegal mass migrations, especially from Haiti. Building partner capacity includes the training and education of foreign military forces.

SOUTHCOM maintains several different forces and organizational structures to perform these missions. Its major components include U.S. Army South (Fort Sam Houston, Texas), the 12th Air Force (Davis-Monthan Air Force Base, Arizona), the U.S. Navy 4th Fleet (Mayport Naval Station, Jacksonville, Florida), U.S. Marine Corps Forces South (Miami, Florida), and Special Operations Command South (Homestead Air Reserve Base, Florida). It maintains several operational structures, including Joint Task Force Bravo in Honduras, Joint Task Force Guantanamo in Cuba, Joint Interagency Task Force South in Key West, Florida, and the William C. Perry Center for Hemispheric Studies in Washington, DC.

According to the Disaster Response Staff Officer's Handbook, "a Joint Task Force (JTF) is constituted and designated by the Secretary of Defense" (CALL 2007, 42). JTFs are a force structure designed after World War II to provide ad hoc military command, control, and coordination for temporary missions (Mandeles 2010). Many have evolved in permanent sub-organizations, such as JTF-Bravo, JTF-Guantanamo, and JIATF-South (which has an interagency designation, since it includes civilian U.S. government agencies like Customs and Border Protection (CBP) and the Drug Enforcement Agency (DEA)) (SOUTHCOM 2014).

A JTF can also be stood up for contingency operations. Such was the case with JTF-Haiti, which was stood up on January 14th, two days after the earthquake. Usually, a JTF is deliberately planned and assembled from well-trained military units.[31] In the case of JTF-Haiti, it was cobbled together rapidly with various units, built from the bottom-up. This occurred largely because Lieutenant General P.K. "Ken" Keen, the deputy commander of SOUTHCOM, happened to be in Haiti for meetings with the U.S. ambassador, and began calling for resources almost immediately. Normally, a different general officer in charge of an operational unit would have been selected to lead the JTF, but Keen was in country, with the ambassador, and had the most knowledge of the "ground truth" regarding the earthquake devastation and needed resources.[32] Additionally, he had a personal relationship with the commanding general in charge of the U.N. MINUSTAH forces in Haiti, a Brazilian officer that he had trained with as a young army captain while on a military-to-military exchange, one of SOUTHCOM's original capacity building missions (Keen 2010, Cecchine et al 2013). SOUTHCOM also established Joint Logistics Command-Haiti to support long-term aid operations.

Some of the resources SOUTHCOM deployed for JTF-Haiti included 60 Marine aircraft, the 18th Airborne Corps' Assault Command Post (ACP), and parts of the 82nd Airborne Division (SOUTHCOM 2014). Additional resources for JTF-Haiti during the

---

[31] Author's interview with a SOUTHCOM officer, 2014.

[32] "Ground truth" is military jargon for actual conditions on the field of battle, vice perceptions back at headquarters.

emergency response phase of the disaster included the USS *Carl Vinson* carrier strike group and parts of the 3rd and 22nd Marine Expeditionary Units. The emergency response phase of the incident continued until February 5, when the military determined it had shifted to what it called "Phase II", relief operations. JTF-Haiti's accomplishments are listed in Table 7.

Support of Humanitarian Assistance and Disaster Relief
- U.S. Military personnel (peak level): 22,268
- U.S. Navy ships: 23
- U.S. Coast Guard ships: 10
- Fixed-wing aircraft: 264
- Helicopters: 57
- Liters of water distributed: 2,600,000
- Humanitarian rations packages distributed: 2,900,000
- Bulk food delivered (pounds): 17,000,000
- Meals-Ready-to-Eat delivered: 2,700,000
- Emergency radios distributed: 73,300
- Hours of emergency radio broadcasts: 660
- Supported distribution of emergency shelter to 1,170,000 people
- Supported 16 World Food Program distribution points.
- Supported development of two transitional camps and improvements in nine camps

Logistical Assistance
- Internally displaced persons (IDP) relocated from high flood risk areas: 3,884
- Number of DoD-coordinated flights into Haiti and neighboring Dominican Republic from January 12 to March 15, 2010: 3,989
- American citizens transported out of Haiti: 16,412
- Air delivered relief (pounds): More than 36 million

Medical Assistance
- U.S. government medical personnel in Haiti (peak level): 1,100
- Number of hospital beds provided (peak level): 1,400
- Number of patients aboard all ships (peak level): 543
- Pounds of medical supplies delivered: 149,045
- Surgeries performed by U.S. military: 1,025
- Medical evacuations: 343
- Patients treated by U.S. military: 9,758

Engineering Assistance
- Number of Haitian engineers trained: 160
- City streets cleared of rubble (cubic yards): 12,724
- Number of structures assessed: (Current as of 23 April 2010): 25,522
- Seaport Flow: Port re-opened on January 22, 2010 with U.S. Military assistance
- Ship containers off-loaded: Twenty-foot Equivalent units (TEU): 8,867

Airport Flow Pre/Post-Earthquake
- Pre-quake average was 20 flights per day
- Post-quake peak capacity of 168 flights in one day
- Airport Timeline:
  - January 13: U.S. Military re-opens airport at request of Government of Haiti and begins 24/7 operations
  - February 18: Government of Haiti begins gradual assumption of air traffic control duties
  - February 19: Commercial flights resume
  - March 16: Government of Haiti resumes full air traffic control of airport

---

Table 7. JTF-HAITI ACTIONS, OPERATION UNIFIED RESPONSE (SOUTHCOM 2014).

SOUTHCOM Humanitarian Assistance/Disaster Response Doctrine

SOUTHCOM is a joint military command that consists of uniformed personnel from all the military branches, civilian Department of Defense employees, and contractors. All military personnel have been indoctrinated through their own branch's boot-camps and officer training programs, and have progressed through operational and staff assignments. It has an inherently insider career ladder. Although personnel do move into and out of the command through their career, they must meet prerequisite rank and experience to serve in specific positions, and the turnover rate is managed to maintain organizational capability. Roles are specifically designated in policy and procedure. It retains a robust, thick military culture, with distinct military processes and procedures for mobilization and deployment of troops through the chain of command.[33]

Military instruction for humanitarian assistance and disaster response is described in the *Disaster Response Staff Officer's Handbook*, focusing on how to respond to a domestic emergency in the United States. While not a formal doctrine, it states that the military must be asked in to help, will play a supporting role, will leave before the local authorities become dependent upon military support, and will follow rules and applicable laws (CALL 2007, 1). International deployments follow analogous principles, but are not clearly articulated in an overarching doctrinal document. Management of specific events around the globe is left to each individual command. The Department of State's ambassador remains the prime authority for U.S. assistance in a foreign country. U.S. code provides authority for the military to provide assistance at the request of a foreign government for both natural and manmade disasters, however the Office of the Secretary of Defense's authorizing polices for HA/DR missions in effect at the time of the Haiti earthquake was dated from 1975, and had not been updated at the time the earthquake struck; it referenced U.S. military organizations that no longer existed (Cecchine et al 2013, 13-15).

In 2008, the SOUTHCOM commander established a unique, non-traditional organizational structure in order to increase its interaction with partners in its AOR. As discussed later, this created challenges during the earthquake when SOUTHCOM had to integrate hundreds of military personnel from other commands into its organization (GAO 2010).

At the time of the earthquake, SOUTHCOM was a thick military culture, with an insider career ladder, and limited workforce autonomy.

---

[33] Author's interview with a military officer, 2014.

Independent Variables	
Paramilitarism	Thick
Career Ladder	Insider
Workforce Autonomy	Low

Table 8. SOUTHCOM INDEPENDENT VARIABLES.

THIS PAGE INTENTIONALLY BLANK

CHAPTER IV. SPEEDING INTO ACTION IN HAITI

This section discusses the initial response of the three selected disaster response organizations to the earthquake, including how they recognized what was happening, responded, organized, and acted. The influence of the independent variables of paramilitarism, career ladders, and workforce autonomy is illustrated through the actions of a USCGC Cutter, the efforts of SOUTHCOM/JTF-Haiti, a FEMA US&R team, IMAT, and FEMA headquarters staff. The processes by which these units received and assessed information, received orders or made decisions, organized and coordinated with others through formal or informal networks or processes, and initiated some sort of activity is presented. This process tracing method attempts to draw parallels and/or distinctions between these different units, correlated to the independent variables that are under examination. An analysis of these actions is presented in the next chapter.

RECOGNIZE

"I knew it was coming because of my experience."

Recognition that an event is occurring or about to occur is the first phase of speeding into action. Weick and others have described the importance of organizational sensemaking to perceive when non-routine events take place (Weick 1993). Earthquakes remain sudden, no-notice events. The U.S. Geological Survey tracks earthquakes around the world and provides an alert and notification service via email and text to subscribers (USGS 2014).

Coast Guard: Aboard USCGC FORWARD, Guantanamo Bay, Cuba

Commander Diane Durham was sitting in her cabin in the late afternoon of January 12, 2010. As commanding officer (CO) of the U.S. Coast Guard Cutter (USCGC) *Forward*, she led a crew of 14 officers and 90 enlisted personnel. The Portsmouth, Virginia-based *Forward* was tied up to the dock at the U.S. Naval Station Guantanamo Bay, Cuba, taking on supplies and conducting minor maintenance work, while on a short stopover from its Windward Passage patrol to deter illegal migration from Haiti and keep an eye out for narcotics traffickers, both routine USCG homeland security missions. Most of the crew was ashore on leave, taking advantage of the naval base hospitality. She expected that many of them were tossing back a few beers.

Durham was taking care of her own administrative duties, awaiting the arrival of the USCGC *Tahoma*, due in port for repairs to its small boats, the deployable rigid-hull inflatable boats (RIBs) used for boarding vessels at sea and various rescue operations. She was a long-time colleague of the *Tahoma*'s CO and they were scheduled to have dinner at the officers' mess in port.

Commander Durham's leadership had been honed over two-decades in the USCG, both at sea and teaching at the USCG Academy: nine of her years of service were spent aboard various cutters on different deployments. Her sailors stated that she endeavored to build a command climate built on "trust and communication" (Tamargo 2011).

Around four in the afternoon, the ship and the dock shook violently. The skeleton crew aboard figured out fairly quickly it must have been an earthquake. Crews ashore felt the quake, as well, and the various TV screens in the base shops, bars, and recreation areas came alive with initial news reports of the very beginnings of an earthquake epicentered in Haiti. She spoke to her crewmembers, giving orders for them to begin taking aboard any emergency supplies that they could get from the U.S. Navy. Their deployment would come hastily, "I knew it was coming because of my experience," she reflected.[34]

The USCGC *Tahoma* arrived, and she met up with its commander for a quick bite to eat and to talk over deployment plans. Simultaneously, the first orders from the USCG chain of command began to arrive. The first was a rapid message from a petty officer at her command, USCG District 7 (D7, in Miami), "Get underway for Haiti." That message was followed by a more specific mission from the District 7 captain, her supervisor on the patrol: get to Port-au-Prince, establish air separation for aircraft, as the airport tower seemed to be off line, and get "eyes on the ground" to report on what was happening. She and the CO of *Tahoma* agreed that *Forward* should make way immediately, and that *Tahoma* would continue to stock up on supplies, while the maintenance crews made the necessary repairs to its RIBs.

---

[34] Author's interview with Captain Diane Durham, March 20, 2014.

Then *Tahoma* would sail in the morning. Durham spoke to two of her senior chiefs, ordering the crew's shore liberty cut short and issuing an emergency recall of all personnel. The crew had already started returning, in surprisingly sober condition for sailors on liberty, perhaps having felt the quake and anticipating the recall themselves. Within a few hours, they were ready to push off under the darkening night sky.

SOUTHCOM: U.S. Ambassador's Residence, Port-au-Prince, Haiti

Lieutenant General P.K. "Ken" Keen was visiting Haiti and had arrived at the residence of the U.S. ambassador, Kenneth Merton. They had a planned dinner. Both were career officers, Keen of the U.S. Army, a former Joint Special Operations Command (JSOC) Green Beret commando with experience in Latin America, Europe and the Middle East, he was now serving as the Deputy Commander of U.S. Southern Command (SOUTHCOM) based out of Miami, Florida. Merton was a member of the U.S. State Department Foreign Service, a career diplomat with service at posts in Europe, Washington, and two prior tours in Haiti, as vice consul and economic counselor (US Army 2009, State Department 2014). This was Merton's first ambassadorial post, the pinnacle of a foreign service officer's (FSO) career.

At 4:53 PM local time the earthquake struck, shaking the ambassador's residence (Cecchine et al 2013). It was obvious that a severe incident had occurred; however, the residence had withstood the quake and partial phone and Blackberry email communications with the Department of State in Washington and with SOUTHCOM in Florida remained intact.

Some of Keen's staff officers were back at the five-story Hotel Montana, where he and the others were staying on their visit. Now it was a collapsed pile of rubble, alongside nearly 100,000 other buildings in the Haitian capital. His desk officer, Lieutenant Colonel Ken Bourland, had been killed in his room on the second floor as the five-story hotel came down in a pile of rubble; another staff member staying on the fifth floor survived, but was injured (Ryan 2013, 5). Within hours, a motorbike arrived at the ambassador's residence carrying a representative of Haitian President René Préval, requesting urgent assistance from the United States (Cecchine et al 2013, 22). One of the first requests from the government of Haiti was to open and take control of the air traffic at Toussaint Louverture International Airport (PAP), the main international airport for the country.

As the ambassador began the process to declare an emergency and release an immediate $50,000 in aid (the maximum authorized amount by the State Department, even if paltry), Keen contacted SOUTHCOM, and immediately began issuing verbal orders of the commanding officer (VOCOs) to his staff in Florida. According to a RAND report, Keen "relied on his judgment as a senior U.S. military commander" (Cecchine et al 2013, 34). In doing so, Keen chose not to wait for the normal process for determining what forces would be necessary, bypassing the usual procedures, which was his prerogative as commanding general.

As the incident unfolded over the first evening of the crisis, the Department of Defense issued a warning order (WARNORD) to SOUTHCOM and the other military commands to begin preparations for humanitarian assistance and disaster response (HA/DR) operations (Cecchine et al 2013, 32). Reports over the first few days through traditional communications channels were very limited; most information was coming through the media. By one account, "there were more members of the media on the ground in Port-au-Prince than U.S. military" (Ryan 2010, 3). The Pentagon bureaucracy would spend the next several weeks trying to get the paperwork to catch up with General Keen's VOCOs.[35]

At Pope Air Force Base in Fayetteville, North Carolina, U.S. Air Force Special Tactics Squadron 21 (21st STS) was preparing for a training exercise when breaking news of the earthquake reached them.[36] A member of the U.S. Air Force Special Operations Command (SOC), the 21st STS is as highly trained as a Navy SEAL team or Army Green Beret A-team. Their pararescuers land behind enemy lines to rescue downed pilots, to direct stealth bomber attacks, and serve as forward air controllers in the most dire of combat situations around the globe.

The 21st STS air traffic control (ATC) expertise was ideally suited towards the needs at Toussaint Louverture International Airport, but they would need orders from SOC to deploy. The unit was already packed for their training exercise, and there was a special operations aircraft on the runway. The commanders of 21st STS began working the phones and email, working up the chain of command to get approval. Their electronic offers of help would quickly be matched to one of Keen's first VOCOs.

FEMA Headquarters, 500 C Street SW, Washington, DC

FEMA is the U.S. government's chief coordinator for domestic emergency management. It maintains a 24-hour watch center for emergencies called the National Response Coordination Center (NRCC), located at FEMA headquarters in Southwest Washington, DC. Emergency managers generally face two kinds of events: slowly developing events such as a hurricane, and rapidly occurring "no notice" events. Despite the best efforts to predict earthquakes, they still remain a "no-notice" emergency.

The Department of the Interior's U.S. Geological Survey (USGS) maintains watch over earthquake activity around the world; hundreds occur daily.[37] They provide an alert service that sends notifications via email or text when they happen.[38] On January 12, 2010, most of the FEMA senior leadership was in Atlanta, Georgia for a "thunderbolt" exercise at FEMA's Region 4 offices. Thunderbolts were the name given to the no-notice spot exercises that FEMA Administrator Craig Fugate had brought with him from Florida, where he had been the state director of emergency management (Ripley 2009, Reilly 2009). Region 4 is one of 10 FEMA regions, and is responsible for the southeast United States.

Tim Manning was the senior FEMA official back in Washington, DC. Deputy Administrator for Protection and National Preparedness, his office had a wide portfolio of grants, prevention, and preparedness programs. He had previously served as the New

---

[35] The official RAND army after action report seemed to both commend the actions of the General, and express frustration that it messed up the usual neat and orderly mustering and deployment of military forces, stating, "General Keen's informal approach to determining initial requirements and his use of VOCOs for force selection and assignment generated a top-down push that resulted in a high volume of people and resources to the relief effort quickly" (Cecchine et al 2013, 64); yet, "the informal, top-down process that pushed resources to the effort so quickly generated inefficiencies that might have impaired the operation's effectiveness." (Cecchine et al 2013, 65).

[36] Author's interview with an Air Force officer, 2014.

[37] USGS maintains the Congressionally established National Earthquake Hazards Reduction Program (http://www.nehrp.gov/) and provides open source earthquake information at http://earthquake.usgs.gov/.

[38] Detailed overviews of the USGS alerting system can be found at http://earthquake.usgs.gov/earthquakes/feed/v1.0/.

Mexico state emergency manager and homeland security advisor, a cabinet-level position that reported to the governor. Earlier in his career, he had been a firefighter, a mountain rescuer, and a geologist for the New Mexico emergency management agency. His Blackberry buzzed with the alert from USGS. He walked down the hall to the NRCC to see if they had it on their radar. "We don't do other countries," one of the watch officer's replied. But Manning thought, "In my gut, we're gonna get sucked into this right away."[39]

Nearby in Fairfax County, Virginia, pagers began alerting the members of Virginia Task Force One (VA-TF1), the Fairfax County Fire and Rescue department urban search and rescue (US&R) team. The Fairfax County team is one of 28 FEMA certified and funded US&R teams in the U.S., and also one of only two teams that is contracted with USAID and certified by the U.N. to deploy to international emergencies.[40] The team consists of firefighters, paramedics, doctors, structural engineers, search dogs, and communications specialists. Battalion Chief Kathleen Stanley was on duty at the fire station when she received her alert to report to the county's fire training academy, the assembly point for VA-TF1. The team had to wait orders to deploy. "We can't do anything until called," Stanley said later.[41]

Anxiety was high as on duty personnel mustered, and off duty personnel collected their team gear and headed for the academy. The team was familiar with Haiti; they had responded there in 2008 when a school collapsed, killing 93 children (REUTERS 2008). They all knew the Haitian building construction techniques were substandard, and knew the faster they got on the ground, the more lives that could be saved. But there was confusion regarding the deployment. Was this a FEMA deployment? Was this a USAID deployment? The team has patches on their uniform sleeves: on the left shoulder is their Fairfax County VA-TF1 team logo; on the right shoulder is a Velcro patch awaiting either a FEMA US&R patch or a USAID USA-1 patch, depending on who is authorizing them to respond. "We probably changed them like six times," said Stanley.[42] The US&R team goals are to deploy within 6 hours by air from an alert (FEMA US&R Strategic Plan 2013). At 6:25 PM, the orders to deploy as USA-1 arrived. Initially, they were ordered to send their normal 72-person "heavy" rescue team, within 24 hours they were also asked to send their 38-person "medium" team, forming a "super-jumbo" task force with six rescue squads and three recon teams (VA-TF1 2010). It would be the first time such a large single US&R task force had been deployed. The team waited overnight at the training academy for further instructions on how they would get to Haiti.

---

[39] Author's interview with a Tim Manning, 2013.
[40] The other USAID is sponsored by the Los Angeles County Fire Department, known as California Task Force 2 (CA-TF2). It is also a FEMA US&R team. Fairfax's US&R team is designated as USA-1 when deployed by USAID, and Los Angeles is designated as USA-2.
[41] Authors interview with Battalion Chief Kathleen Stanley, 2014.
[42] Ibid.

RESPOND

"The bureaucracy was eliminated by this approach."[43]

Response is both the physical and administrative phase of speeding into action, to include the deployment of personnel, approval of orders and missions, and the logistical movement of necessary materials and supplies to the location of the emergency.

Coast Guard: Aboard the USCGC FORWARD, Gulf of Gonâve

The USCGC *Forward* had made a hasty departure from U.S. Naval Station Guantanamo Bay, getting underway at night and without the benefit of "track lines down," the lexicon for the detailed computer navigation that would have carefully guided the ship via GPS waypoints towards Port-au-Prince. But speed demanded a few shortcuts. Over the night, Commander Durham pondered her ship's mission. As they drew towards the shores of Haiti, her looming fear was coming across a migrant Haitian boat. Haitian migrants were know for packing hundreds of people on boats in an effort to reach the U.S. by sea, and the earthquake might have made them more desperate; they were also know for swarming from one side of the boat towards USCGC vessels that intercepted them, occasionally capsizing the vessels and tossing the Haitians into the ocean. "That won't play well in *The Washington Post*," Durham thought as *Forward* made its way Southeasterly across the Windward Passage.[44]

Shortly after dawn the morning after the earthquake, *Forward* arrived at Port-au-Prince, approaching without the usual benefit of a harbor pilot. The ships crew navigated carefully past some debris in the bay. Durham's concern about a group of migrants swarming the ship was replaced by the immediate concern of careful navigation. She maintained a vigil from the pilothouse; only later in the day would her crew tell her that hundreds of Haitians ashore were cheering their arrival. In addition to the flotsam littering the water, the bay reeked with the pungent odor of spilled fuel. As a fire safety measure, Durham order the smoking lamps put out, and the *Forward* anchored in the harbor.[45] It was time to get to work. She launched the *Forward*'s helicopter to conduct a quick assessment of the capital and check on the conditions at the airport.

USCG air stations from Clearwater and Alabama sortied many aircraft, including MH-65 Dolphin and MH-60 Jayhawk helicopters, C-130 Hercules airplanes, and the USCG's newest HC-144A Ocean Sentry airplanes. The aircraft flew grid patterns to assess damage, search for survivors, and to evacuate American citizens and the injured (Johnson 2010, Tamargo 2011). At its peak, the USCG had eight cutters and over 800 personnel supporting the Haitian relief effort. USCG Commandant Thad Allen also recalled 900 USCG reservists to duty to enhance security operations in Port-au-Prince (USCG Secretary Napolitano 2010). There was no centralized USCG command element; instead, the USCG ships conducted a series of decentralized actions to address a wide spectrum of emergency needs.

---

[43] Ryan 2010, 8

[44] Author's interview with Captain Diane Durham, March 20, 2014.

[45] The "smoking lamp" is a nautical term used to describe when it is safe for mariners for smoke at sea. Many ships indicate when smoking is permitted by illuminating a smoking sign; smoking is not permitted when it is turned off.

SOUTHCOM: U.S. Embassy, Port-au-Prince, Haiti

The devastation was becoming evident to General Keen and Ambassador Merton and their staffs. Keen had lost one of his aides in the quake. The civilian head and the chief deputy of the U.N. mission in Haiti had been killed in the collapse of their headquarters. A total of 101 U.N. personnel were killed, the largest number of deaths in a single event in U.N. history. Keen reached out to MINUSTAH, establishing contact with its senior military officer, Major General Floriano Peixoto Vieira Neto of Brazil. They had known each other since they were young captains, conducting joint military-to-military training and exercises in Brazil when Keen was assigned on a military exchange during his career development in the U.S. Army.

The two generals met on the morning of January 13 at Toussaint Louverture International Airport (PAP) to inspect the runway and check on the air tower. Keen continued to issue VOCOs, calling for a U.S. Air Force special operations detachment to take control of the airport, which his staff deemed serviceable. The shipping port was severely damaged and had yet to be assessed, the roads were either impassible or clogged with survivor traffic, leaving the airport as the key to establishing a supply chain in and out of the country. Keen also knew he'd need command and control, as well as immediate help, so he called on the deployment of the Global Response Force (GRF), a standby unit ready for deployment to combat anywhere in the world within 96 hours; the GRF unit on call January 13 was the 82nd Airborne's 2nd Brigade Combat Team at Fort Bragg, North Carolina, some 1,200 miles away (Tan 2013, Cecchine et al 2013). He also called upon the headquarters element of the 18th Airborne Corps to respond and set up command and coordination, initially at the U.S. embassy, and then at with the remnants of the MINSUTAH forces (Cecchine et al 2013). Keen ordered SOUTHCOM to continue to send forces forward until he said stop; an admiral serving as the SOUTHCOM operations officer (J-3) stated, "We had 16 pages of VOCOs regarding force flow. Official RFFs [requests for forces] were not required and the bureaucracy was eliminated by this approach. This was the enabler for speed of response" (Ryan 2010, 8).

In the meantime, Major General Floriano Peixoto of MINUSTAH talked his way aboard a USCG helicopter that had landed to survey the Toussaint Louverture International Airport, and took to the sky to do a visual damage assessment of the city. It was the beginning of a military mobilization that would bring aid from over 20 foreign militaries, supporting the response of over 140 countries and 500-1000 NGOs (Ryan 2010). The Pentagon designated the event as Operation Unified Response (OUR), and at the peak of response there were over 22,000 U.S. military personnel, 33 naval vessels, and 41 aircraft working to rescue, feed, shelter, and aid the 1.7 million Haitian earthquake survivors (JCOA 2010). Coordinating those forces would fall to General Keen, and on January 14th he assumed command of Joint Task Force - Haiti (JTF-Haiti), the command structure SOUTHCOM decided to establish to direct all U.S. military forces in OUR (Cecchine et al 2013).

Back at Pope Air Force Base, the 21st STS was working up their chain of command to get approval to deploy. This was a rare effort for a lower echelon unit to seek permission by working up the bureaucracy. Limited aircraft were available, but they had been ready to begin a training mission with an elite USAF special operations C130 crew; these were the world's best aviators, from the same special operations squadrons that would later fly top secret stealth helicopters into Pakistan for the raid on Osama Bin Laden's compound.

As the STS leaders made an agreement with the C130 crew to divert from their training mission to Toussaint Louverture International Airport, the chain of command finally caught up and issued their orders. On January 13th, a day after the earthquake they were airborne. It would require a night landing on a runway in unknown condition, exactly what they trained to do every day.[46]

FEMA: The White House, Washington, DC, (One Day After Earthquake)

Overnight on January 12, many moving parts started into motion. FEMA senior staff returned to Washington from Atlanta, and Administrator Fugate attended a meeting at The White House with the President's cabinet and other senior White House staff. President Obama was clear that he wanted the red tape cut and a whole of government response.[47] USAID was by statute the lead federal agency, but the USAID administrator was only days in office, and many of the disaster response positions were still unfilled (USAID 2013, Cecchine 2013). As the president polled his cabinet for resources that could be used in Haiti, USCG Commandant Thad Allen suggesting putting FEMA communications and staff on a Coast Guard C130 to provide essential support to the ambassador, drawing on his experience from Hurricane Katrina. Allen saw the earthquake as a weapon of mass effect that had incapacitated the local governing authorities, mirroring the effect of Hurricane Katrina in Louisiana.[48] Fugate offered up FEMA's mobile emergency response support (MERS) units, one of its incident management assistance teams (IMAT), and its additional US&R teams to support the USAID effort.[49] The FEMA US&R teams had never before been deployed outside the U.S. Eventually, eight teams were activated, and four responded, in addition to the two USAID teams.[50]

IMAT-West was activated to respond. One of three national IMATs, their missions are often the biggest and most complex, from designated National Special Security Events (NSSE) like the Super Bowl to storms like Hurricane Sandy. Their purpose on a domestic incident is to bring coordination of all federal resources, a roving staff for whoever is designated at the Federal Coordinating Officer (FCO). The teams were developed out of the lessons from Hurricane Katrina, and codified in the Post Katrina Emergency Management Reform Act (Congress *PKEMRA* 2006). But that was inside the U.S., and this was its first international mission, an overlapping role with USAID's Disaster Assistance Response Teams (DART), which handle overseas crisis coordination for the Department of State. The leaders of the IMAT were told to "figure it out when they got there."[51] The team leader reached out to his staff to notify them of their assignment; one member's reply was, "You're kidding -- it's foreign!"[52]

---

[46] Author's interview with a member of the 21st STS, 2014.

[47] Author's interview with a senior FEMA official, 2013.

[48] Author's interview with Admiral Thad Allen, 2013.

[49] The MERS units are spread around the U.S., basically big satellite and communications trucks and teams that can go into a disaster area to reestablish field communications. MERS units from Maryland, Georgia, and Massachusetts were deployed (Legeros 2010). They are flown routinely on USCG C-130 aircraft. IMATs are FEMA's teams for coordinating field operations, logistics, and planning using the incident command system (ICS).

[50] Those additional US&R teams included NY-TF1 (New York City Fire Department, New York), VA-TF2 (Virginia Beach Fire Department, Virginia), FL-TF1 (Miami Dade Fire and Rescue, Florida), and the FL-TF2 (City of Miami Fire Rescue, Florida). TX-TF1 (College Station, Texas), CA-TF5 (Orange County Fire Department, California), CA-TF7 (Sacramento Fire Department, California), and OH-TF1 (Dayton Fire Department, OH) were all alerting, mobilized, and then stood down prior to flying to Haiti.

[51] Author's interview with an IMAT member, 2014.

[52] Ibid.

Meanwhile, VA-TF1/USA-1 was loading their equipment by hand onto a commercial airplane at Washington Dulles International Airport (IAD). Normally, they had an MOU (memorandum of understanding) with the U.S. military to fly their 72-person team, rescue equipment, trucks, and dogs from Andrews Air Force Base in nearby Maryland to wherever they were deployed. All their equipment and supplies had been pre-measured, weighed, palletized, and practiced for loading onto a USAF C-130 aircraft. But there was a shortage of military airframes; two wars and General Keen's hasty call for aid had rerouted a lot of military flights. They also had more equipment and personnel in their ad hoc "super jumbo" task force organization. Additionally, they had heard the runway at Port-au-Prince's Toussaint Louverture International Airport was not operational. VA-TF1 was using plan B, their MOU with a commercial carrier, which meant they had to load the plane's cargo hold with rescue gear, tents, generators, and everything they'd need to be self-sustaining for two weeks all by themselves; no easy loading of pallets by expert USAF logistics staff, and more importantly, no room to load their trucks. It would be up to the commercial airline pilots to find a runway in Haiti or the Dominican Republic. The task force members would then have to find transport on the ground in Haiti. At least they'd have a bathroom on the flight, unlike IMAT West, which on January 14 was being loaded onto a bathroom-less Coast Guard C-130 in California for the cross-country flight to Homestead Air Force Base, Florida, a stopover to receive inoculations and a medical exam from U.S. government physicians, and then on to Haiti.[53]

Over the next few days, senior staff White House and FEMA tried to get a handle on what was happening, how to get the U.S. involved, and how to coordinate this new "whole of government" concept. Over the first week, the staff got fragmented orders as the Deputy National Security Advisor started issuing simple commands: as the week evolved, those orders went from "Go help Raj" [Shah, the new head of USAID], to "Go to SOUTHCOM," then eventually, "Go to Haiti," and finally "Go fix it."[54] Without an organizing construct for blending the domestic and international response mechanisms, the White House and U.S. government leadership was forced to improvise in an effort to speed the whole government into action.

---

[53] Quoted one IMAT member, "all everyone on the team wanted was a rest room." Author's interview with IMAT member, 2014.

[54] Author's interview with a senior government official, 2013.

ORGANIZE

"I kept asking who was running the response, and the answer was USAID. We never saw 'em."[55]

Organization is an essential administrative function, noted in the fields founding traditions (Gulick 1937). The organizing phase of speeding into action is when the formal and informal processes of command, control, and coordination are established.

COAST GUARD: USCGC FORWARD, Port-au-Prince Harbor

The *Forward*'s crew was picking up communications from different sources, including the U.S. embassy, and began an effort to pass information up its chain of command, first to USCG 7th District ("D7", in Miami), and then onto Atlantic Area Command in Portsmouth. Durham had worked for four years at Atlantic Area Command, including a stint as Assistant to the Chief of Operations during Hurricane Katrina, when she was involved in the direction of USCG air and ship assets in response to the storm. Those assets were credited with rescuing over 33,500 people during the hurricane, the largest rescue in American history, and widely considered the U.S. Coast Guard's finest moment (GAO 2006). She knew they would be clamoring for information to feed the chain of command. It was part a "brief-up" culture that existed the higher up one went in the chain of command.[56] The further from the action, the greater that action was replaced with an insatiable desire for information.

USCGC *Mohawk* was the second U.S. ship to arrive on January 13th. Its officer was junior in rank to Durham, so she automatically assumed the role of CTU, or commander of the task unit. She reflected later, "I kept asking who was running the response, and the answer was USAID. We never saw 'em."[57]

Additional cutters arrived and fell under the CTU, including the USCGC *Valiant*. Their crews prepared to go to work triaging, treating, and transporting survivors, using flight decks to conduct supply drops and transfer patients in their helicopters. The buoy tender USCGC *Oak* arrived and was ordered to begin clearing debris in the harbor (Morrissey 2010).

SOUTHCOM: JTF-HAITI, U.S. Embassy, Port-au-Prince

While the statutory authority for President Barack Obama's orders of a "whole of government" approach to disaster fell to USAID to coordinate, the military retained control of its responding forces through its chain of command. In order to support that military hierarchy, a series of organizational structures were established or adapted to support the rapid and escalating response.

On January 13, 2010, the day after the earthquake, the Chairman of the Joint Chiefs of Staff, Admiral Mike Mullen, sent execution orders (EXORD) to SOUTHCOM to establish a task force to lead the Pentagon's response to the earthquake (Cecchine et al 2013). SOUTHCOM moved to establish a joint forces headquarters (JFHQ) in Port-au-Prince. When Secretary of Defense Robert Gates ordered Operation Unified Response to commence on January 14, this JFHQ morphed into the beginning of JTF-Haiti, with General Keen at the helm. A JTF is an inherently ad hoc organizational structure for crisis response that the military has been using since after World War II (Mandeles 2010, 21).

---

[55] Author's interview with a Coast Guard officer, 2014.
[56] Author's interview with Captain Diane Durham, March 20, 2014.
[57] Ibid.

It would be six weeks before all the operating elements for JTF-Haiti could be mustered into place (Ryan 2010, 5). Part of this delay was the decision by the Joint Staff (the military officers that staff the joint service chiefs at the Pentagon) to deploy a readily available and trained JTF unit, U.S. Army South (ARSOUTH), to Guantanamo Bay, Cuba to serve as a JTF for migrant operations instead of deploy to Port-au-Prince. The Joint Staff was concerned that the earthquake would lead to a mass migration of Haitian refugees to the U.S., and ARSOUTH had plans in place for this mission; therefore they became JTF-Migrant Ops (Ryan 2010, 6). Other readily trained JTF units were already deployed to the Central Command (CENTCOM) in the Middle East. Keen and SOUTHCOM were forced to build their JTF by cobbling together other military units. Eventually, Keen received a phone call from a long-time friend, Lieutenant General Frank Helmick, commander of the 18th Airborne Corps at Fort Bragg, offering to send his Assault Command Post (ACP) and top staff (Ryan 2010, 6). Keen had the nucleus of his JTF-Haiti command and control (C2) organization on the way.

General Keen and General Floriano Peixoto of MINUSTAH agreed that they should keep their coordinating force structures separate; the development of a more elaborate Coalition Joint Task Force (CJTF, combining U.S. and U.N. forces) would have slowed the response down as multiple nations became integrated into the command structure, and potentially confused the role and credibility of MINUSTAH, which had been on the ground since 2004. The U.N.'s MINUSTAH forces would continue their primary mission of security, for which they were originally established, and the U.S. would focus on humanitarian assistance and disaster response. They would remain separate but coordinate (RAND 2013, 389). Given the lack of clear command authority from the U.N., U.S., or Haitian government, it also avoided one old friend from having to subordinate another in the midst of a crisis, a potential political and personal disaster of its own.

Normally, prior to a HA/DR mission, a combat command like SOUTHCOM would send a Humanitarian Assistance Strike Team (HAST) to assess the needs in an area; this would be analogous to a USAID Disaster Assistance Response Team (DART), which does a similar mission for USAID's OFDA (Cecchine et al 2013, 33-34). However, General Keen was already on site, and had access to the embassy telephones. He used his limited communications to set up a series of conference calls with other U.S. generals, marshaling the forces he felt could be of most use (Cecchine et al 2013).

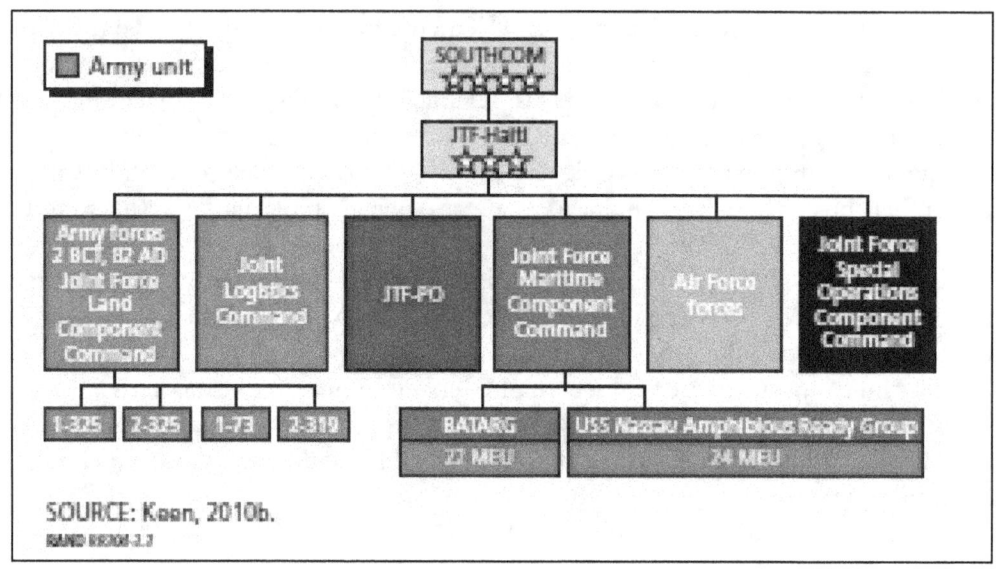

Figure 7. JTF-HAITI ORGANIZATION (Cecchine et al 2013, 37).

JTF-Haiti started work out of the U.S. embassy, facilitating coordination with other U.S. agencies as they arrived and went to work.   Eventually, the JTF grew into its own separate headquarters, and built ties with the reconstituting MINUSTAH forces, and with the U.N. clusters as they were established.

As the demands on JTF-Haiti increased to handle the surge of forces, it established a Humanitarian Assistance Coordination Center (HACC), with personnel split between the embassy and the U.N clusters. As requests for assistance (RFAs) came in from different places, the HACC would process those requests. First, as mission needs presented themselves, they would be entered by USAID into a Mission Tasking Matrix (MITAM); second, the MITAM would then be processed by the HACC for JTF-Haiti; third, JTF-Haiti produced a military order (known as a fragmentary order), which, fourth, was tasked to one of the U.S. military resources with a specific mission. Figure 8 illustrates this process. Eventually, the RFAs were routed through the U.N., because members of the NGOs and the U.N. had trouble gaining access to the HACC at the U.S. embassy (Cecchine et al 2013). In one after action report, the RFA process using the MITAMs was reported as "not responsive enough" (Cecchine et al 2013, 45-46). Another stated:

> Two weeks after the Haitian earthquake, JTF-H still did not have processes in place to match relief needs with arriving supplies. Force flow was ad hoc and based on verbal orders; supporting commands did not communicate adequately with each other about what forces and materiel were transported to Haiti. Ad hoc organization of logistics resulted in speedy, but uncoordinated sequencing of units and equipment (Mandeles 2010, 27).

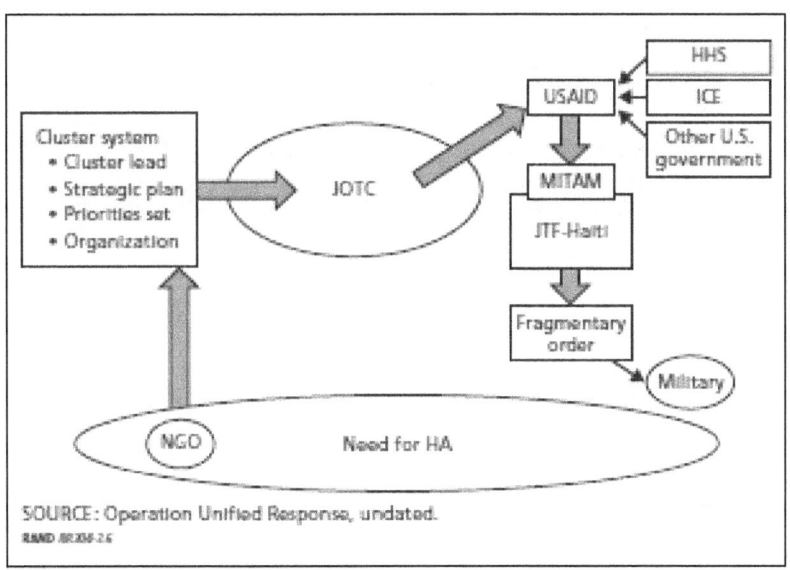

Figure 8. REQUEST FOR ASSISTANCE (RFA) PROCESS, U.S. MILITARY (Cecchine et al 2013, 46).

By January 19, one week after the earthquake, JTF-Haiti had grown to 78 personnel; by January 27, it had 355 personnel and was conducted operations around the clock (Ryan 2010, 7).

The higher echelons were having some challenges keeping up, too. In Miami, SOUTHCOM was struggling with integrating military personnel called in from elsewhere around the globe (GAO 2010). In 2008, SOUTHCOM had replaced its "J-code" organizational structure, adopting a non-traditional organizational structure, one that fit very well with its ongoing military-to-military training in Latin America and the Caribbean, and with its military-to-law enforcement counternarcotic missions (Ryan 2010, 1).[58] Figure 9 illustrates SOUTHCOMs organizational structure prior to the earthquake. This structure was different than the other combat commands around the world, and newly arriving surge of nearly 300 military personnel had trouble understanding it; furthermore, it lacked the operations, logistics, and future planning elements necessary for warfighting, and Haiti had become analogous to a battle (GAO 2010; Ryan 2010, 2). Five days into the disaster response, General Douglas Fraser, commander of SOUTHCOM, ordered an overnight change its organizational structure to fit the traditional structure of a combat command at

---

[58] Ubiquitous among western military commands is a force structure that divides staff work by functional alphabetized and numbered groups. The alphabet, in this case a "J", denotes that it is a "joint" billet that can be filled by a roster of qualified individuals from any military service. The numbers 1 through 9 are fairly universal, 1 for personnel, 2 for intelligence, 3 for operations, 4 for logistics, 5 for plans and strategy, 6 for communications, 7 for training, 8 for resources and assessment, and 9 for partnering. While there are many ways of organizing, in this case the familiarity of this lexicon among military personnel facilitates a "plug and play" force structure for expeditionary forces; nevertheless, it creates a huge headache when trying to integrate between civilian and military organizations, especially civilian organizations using the Incident Command System (ICS) structures, or, as in the case of Haiti, the U.N. cluster system (author's personal observations, 2005 during Hurricane Katrina and 2010 during the Haiti earthquake response).

war, which was welcomed enthusiastically by the staff (Ryan 2010, 5).[59] Figure 10 illustrates this traditional, flatter organizational structure.

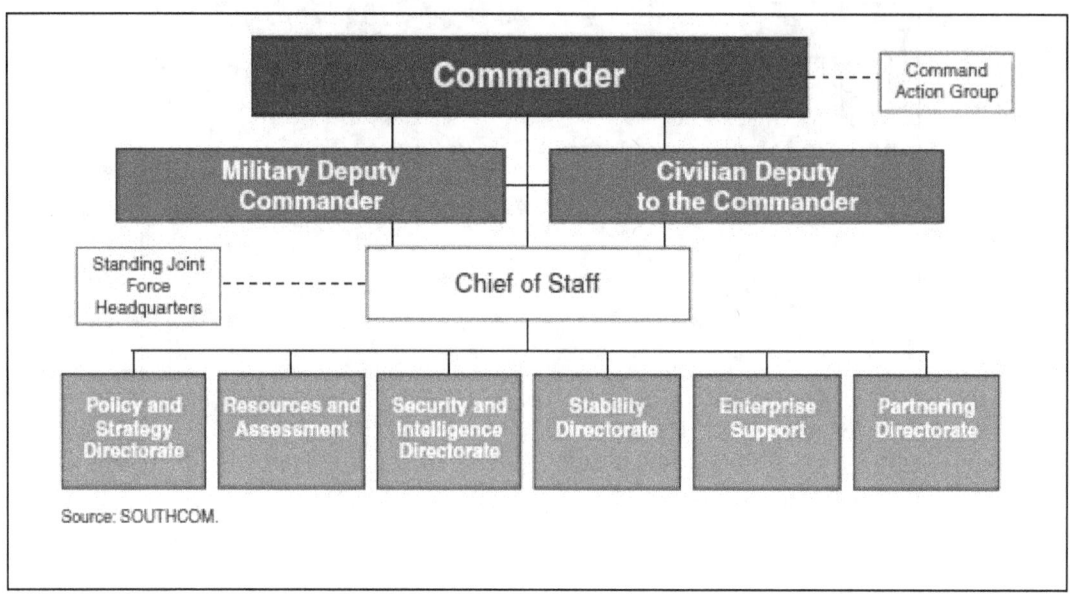

Figure 9. SOUTHCOM "ENTERPRISE" ORGANIZATIONAL STRUCTURE 2008-2010 (GAO 2010, 22).

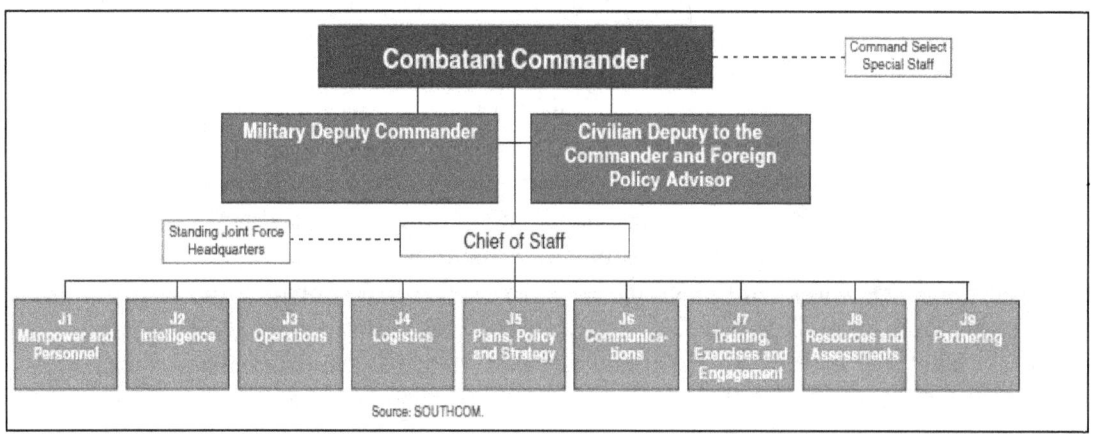

Figure 10. SOUTHCOM "TRADITIONAL" ORGANIZATIONAL STRUCTURE AS ADOPTED DURING OPERATION UNIFIED RESPONSE 2010 (GAO 2010, 29).

---

[59] General Fraser had been commander of SOUTHCOM for 6 months, and coincidentally had discussed with his senior staff concerns over the SOUTHCOM enterprise structure a few days prior to the earthquake (Ryan 2010, 5).

FEMA: VA-TF1/USA-1 B.O.O. (Base Of Operations), End of the runway, Toussaint-Louverture International Airport (PAP)

VA-TF1 had made it to Port-au-Prince in two stages. Its "heavy" rescue team had arrived the evening of January 13th; Chief Stanley and the smaller "medium" rescue team had arrived at 5:00 AM on the 14th. It was the first time both groups had been deployed at the same time. The airport had been reopened, and they had unloaded their supplies and rescue gear. They spent one day at the airport, and then moved to the embassy to set up their base of operations (BOO). Early into their arrival, they had bumped into an Air Force unit that had established air traffic control (ATC) for the airport. It was easy to find them, they were working from a fold-up card table at the end of the runway, using portable radios to direct the airplanes landing and taking off. A few of the USAF guys were hunting for the ability to do something -- they were pararescuers trained as medics to save trapped pilots from downed planes and helicopters. They had initially provided some security for their fellow airmen who specialized in ATC operations, but those guys were well into their own mission, and the pararescuers knew there were other needs in the destroyed city. VA-TF1 was happy to have them, they'd provide some security, and, most importantly, they had a Humvee. They first set off with the Task Force's communications (comms) personnel.

That was the protocol for the US&R team: get the BOO up, get the comms established, find who needs to be rescued, and go to work. It looked like their first mission would be to a place called the Hotel Montana; there were reports that many Americans were trapped there, and the US&R team would need to improvise a command structure to manage their medium and heavy rescue team operations, something they had never done before.

FEMA's IMAT had arrived on third day after the earthquake, and was getting settled into the U.S. embassy as well. "We were trying to get a sense of why we were there, what we were doing," said one team member.[60] They had been augmented with the U.S. Coast Guard's Deployable Operations Group (DOG), including a two-star admiral, and several FEMA headquarters staffers, as an ad hoc DHS Integrated Response Team (IRT). Only 25 percent of FEMA's workforce had deployed to disasters in the past four years, Hurricane Katrina having been the last "all hands on deck" incident -- and one that had tarnished the agency's image badly. However, a small percentage of FEMA staff had deployed to over 50 events, and these folks staffed the IMAT. Post-Katrina had left FEMA as a Balkanized, feudal society, and these IMAT personnel were the core trying very hard to rebuild its operational capacity.[61]

One challenge they faced was a lack of clear mission and reporting relationships. Damon Penn was the most senior FEMA official sent "downrange" and led the IRT. He was greeted reluctantly by Ambassador Merton, whose embassy was beginning to look like a KOA campground with U.S. military and civilian responders, and embassy staff that felt safer sleeping in their offices than in their own homes, if they still were standing.[62] Penn, a former Army colonel, was a trusted member of Craig Fugate's team; they had worked together when he was Defense Coordinating Officer (DCO) for FEMA Region 4, during the 2004 hurricane season that ravaged Florida. He did have an assigned mission, "go down and figure out what is going on."

---

[60] Author's interview with IMAT member, 2014.
[61] Author's interview with senior FEMA official, 2013.
[62] Author's interviews with FEMA personnel, 2013 and 2014. "Downrange" is military lexicon for the target area.

The first few days, the team felt like they were meeting "all the wrong people" as they attempted to get organized; it took a few days to figure out that while the ambassador was the lead for the U.S. government, the Chief of Mission really ran the embassy.[63] The USAID Disaster Assistance Response Team (DART) was functioning, and seemed reluctant to accept any immediate help from FEMA. International disaster response has long relied on the humanitarian ethos, whereas FEMA had been learning since Katrina to behave more like a fire department; one U.S. official summed up the distinction, "you [FEMA] bring food; we [USAID] bring seeds."[64]

The relationships would warm up over the next couple of weeks, as FEMA supplied food and water for the embassy, the MERS unit created a robust communications conduit, and the staff figured out Penn had a direct line back to Washington without having to go through the State Department. As one FEMA leader stated, "I knew where they [the DART personnel] drink beer every night." It just took some relationship-building to wear down the organizational silos. Once the embassy personnel figured out that the 2-star Coast Guard admiral worked for Penn, his stature increased. The unformed military presence helped calm everyone, "Seeing uniforms, seeing organization -- all helped," he reflected.[65] Thirty U.S. Marines protected the embassy from up to 10,000 Haitians that had gathered around the fence as the IRT staff worked.

The FEMA personnel had been used to clear roles and responsibilities in their domestic mission, and this was an adjustment. In the U.S. at a large disaster, when problems were identified, they'd be assigned by the IMAT to the most appropriate resource to address it. Here in Haiti, the U.N. cluster system was slow to coalesce, the Haitian government was weak, and the U.S. lacked clear authority. Other than the knowledge that they all worked for the Ambassador, the FEMA staff were hampered by the size of event, the velocity of requests, and the ambiguity of their authority. One senior FEMA leader was sent to Haiti, received an uncertain welcome, returned to Miami, and then was ordered back to Haiti to "figure it out when you get there."[66]

Over the next several weeks, organization was aligned around the clusters with the various NGOs. Problems would be presented in "all their gory detail," and the staff would have to wait to see who would "pony up" with a solution. The Department of State sent Ambassador Lewis Lucke, an experienced diplomat, to become the U.S. Response Coordinator for the Haiti earthquake and assist Ambassador Merton. Ambassador Lucke's arrival helped; he immediately garnered acceptance and respect of the USAID and State Department staff, and gave the military's JTF-Haiti staff their desired chain of command to a civilian decision-maker. There were many groups, but no singular person in charge until Lucke arrived. The White House and military personnel eventually put together a tripartite leadership group with a Haitian minister, FEMA leader, and a U.N. representative, who reported up to a governing committee with Haitian President Préval, Ambassador Lucke, and General Keen.[67]

---

[63] Author's interview with senior FEMA official, 2013.
[64] Ibid
[65] Ibid.
[66] Ibid
[67] Author's interviews with senior FEMA and White House staff, 2013 and 2014.

ACT

"We couldn't wait for higher orders."[68]

Action, the actual provision of lifesaving aid, food, shelter, and medical care in response to an emergency, is the ultimate goal of any DRO. As previously discussed, the speed at which action takes place is essential to effective disaster response.

USCGC FORWARD, at Haiti Coast Guard pier, Port-au-Prince

A Haitian Coast Guard vessel came along the USCGC *Forward*, providing the crew with the first real information on the extent of the devastation. The Haitian Coast Guard was also a victim of the quake itself, with its base damaged, some of its members killed, and many others unable to report for duty due to the damaged roadways and lack of transportation throughout the city and nearby areas.

USCG has enjoyed a long history of training and exercising with the Haitian guardsmen, and they were welcome partners. The military-to-military exchanges were smooth, based upon these past relationships, and the shared understanding of each other's roles and chain of command. The Haitians may have spoken French Creole, and the Americans English, but they shared the common guardsmen's language.

The crew of the *Forward* commenced with their initial missions, to support air traffic control (ATC) and to begin to survey the extent of the damage. The ATC systems at the Port-au-Prince international airport had been destroyed in the earthquake. An older cutter commissioned in 1990, the *Forward* lacked the avionic radar systems that modern cutters and most naval vessels possessed.[69] Numerous flights were in the air already. USCG C-130 airplanes were flying video missions, attempting to gain a damage assessment; the USCG had previously negotiated overflight authorization with the Haitian government. Other international, military, and private aircraft were also flying. The *Forward*'s crew improvised, used a tactic called "air separation" to keep planes spaced properly, communicating by radio with aircraft to safely divide the air space into different sectors, even though they had no means of visually tracking each aircraft on radar.[70]

USCG cutters are equipped with helicopters, and Commander Durham launched the *Forward*'s MH-65 Dolphin helicopter, first to assess the airport, and then to get attempt to get a broader damage assessment. Durham also launched *Forward*'s two rigid hull inflatable boats (RIBs): the first boat took a few members of the crew, including interpreter and intelligence officer, to the Haitian Coast Guard base. The second RIB investigated the harbor, looking for places where supply ships might be able to tie up and deliver goods.

Over the first few days, Durham concentrated her ship's efforts on establishing a picture of available supply routes, by sea and by land. The devastation was near apocalyptic. Fires burned from debris and ruptured gas lines across the city. The helicopter was used to assess which roads were passable. "If there were trucks moving, we assumed the road was good," she reflected.[71] Her crew expressed a desire to go ashore and dig through debris for

---

[68] Author's interview with Captain Diane Durham, 2014.
[69] The history of the USCGC *Forward* can be found at www.uscg.mil/lantarea/cgcForward/facts.asp

[70] Author's interview with a Coast Guard officer, 2014.
[71] Author's interview with Captain Diane Durham, March 20, 2014.

survivors, but she determined that the greater good would be served by establishing long-term supply lines for relief. They followed her orders, something that might not have been as easy without the military discipline that flowed from the chain of command. Data about the road networks that they gathered was passed onto the U.S. military's Transportation Command, TRANSCOM.

Helicopters also began flying patients, first to the cutters as they arrived, then to alternate hospitals, and eventually to the USS *Comfort*, the Navy's hospital ship which had sailed from Baltimore. The *Forward* and *Mohawk* were joined by the USCGC *Tahoma*, arriving with the supplies from the naval station at Guantanamo Bay. Durham assigned the *Tahoma*'s commander to take charge of shore operations from the Haitian coast guard base; fortuitously, he had previously served as the USCG liaison to Haiti on a prior U.S. Coast Guard career assignment.

Mohawk's crew assumed air traffic control (ATC) duties from the *Forward*, continuing to maintain the airspace above the country until a U.S. Air Force Special Operations team arrived with special equipment and training to take over the airport's air traffic control after a few days. *Forward* continued to provide refueling for helicopter operations, including six USCG HH-60 Jayhawk helicopters called in to assist from a drug interdiction base in the Bahamas.

The *Forward*'s crew took liberty with USCG policy: early on the first day, the *Forward*'s helicopter had picked up the commanding general in charge of the MINUSTAH forces, and gave him a tour of the island, a violation of policy by taking a foreign dignitary aboard without authorization. "Lot's of things we did and asked for forgiveness later," stated Durham.[72] As medical supplies ran short, they improvised, literally pulling the ship apart for spare fragments of plastic, wood, and metal that could form makeshift splits for the countless injured, providing spare fresh water and damage control tools to their Haitian Coast Guard counterparts, and doing whatever they could to help the suffering.

"We couldn't wait for higher orders," said Durham. Too much needed to get done as resources began to flood into the area. Her crew overheard a radio transmission from the USS *Comfort* to one of the helicopter crews, stating that no Haitian children should be transported to the ship without permission from their parents, or without bringing their parents along because as minors the Navy could not treat them. "Their parents are dead. These kids are orphans," replied an unidentified USCG helicopter pilot.[73] The U.S. Navy hospital ship would be forced to set aside its paperwork routine.

After about a week, the chain of command began to catch up with the USCG task force: helicopter MEDEVACs began to be interspersed with VIP flights and the delivery of food and supplies to responders. From Miami, D7 began issuing orders for personnel to assist the U.S. embassy with evacuation of American citizens. A USCG captain relieved Durham as CTU, and she and the *Forward* crew returned to migrant patrol operations while *Tahoma* and *Mohawk* remained in the harbor. Falling under SOUTHCOM's growing presence, they began to be sent on "wild goose chases" after everything afloat; Durham drafted a special intelligence brief for SOUTHCOM so that they would stop sending the *Forward* after every ferry transiting the gulf. SOUTHCOM didn't have experience in dealing with Haitian migrants, and couldn't distinguish between the routine ferry service on the

---

[72] Author's interview with Captain Diane Durham, March 20, 2014.
[73] Author's interview with Captain Diane Durham, March 20, 2014.

island and the occasional migrant flotilla. The Navy's presence crowded the sea lanes. At one point, the *Forward* was warned off as a Navy vessel radioed to impose a 10-mile exclusion zone around its ships and the aircraft carrier USS *Carl Vinson*, a routine force protection security measure. Durham radioed the Navy vessel, telling them they would be ignoring the exclusion zone, as it occupied all the navigable waters outside the harbor, preventing the entrance of all the international shipping coming in with lifesaving supplies.

Operations continued on a round-the-clock basis: patrolling, fueling, ferrying passengers and supplies via helicopter for over two weeks. On Sunday, January 31, *Forward* sailed into Guantanamo Bay for their first rest in three weeks, just in time for Durham's crew to resume their previously shortened shore liberty, and in time to watch Drew Brees and the New Orleans Saints win Super Bowl XLIV over Peyton Manning and the Indianapolis Colts.

SOUTHCOM: *Toussaint Louverture International Airport, Port-au-Prince, Haiti*

On January 14th, 2010, members of the USAF 21st STS were touching down on the tarmac at Toussaint Louverture International Airport in a USAF Special Operations Command C130. The pilots had made three passes overhead first to visually inspect the runway before risking the landing. The mission for the 21st STS was to establish control of the airspace above Haiti and to get flights moving in and out of the airport; 28 minutes after their feet hit the ground they were broadcasting (Cecchine et al 2013). Over the next day, they took over all ATC duties from USCGC *Mohawk*.[74]

Within a few days, full-scale operations were commencing on all fronts. Flights into and out of the airport went from as little as 20 per day to between 60 and 200 as the ATC system was rebuilt and coordination efforts with other relief agencies grew (Ryan 2010, 7; Mandeles 2010, 28). At its peak, the 21st STS was directing the landing and takeoff of one aircraft every four minutes. They would continue this pace without an accident, near miss, or mishap until relieved by regular USAF ATC personnel.[75]

The aircraft carrier USS *Carl Vinson* (CVN-70) arrived on January 15, and its carrier strike group flew helicopter sorties, dropping supplies, and evacuating medical patients to hospitals across Haiti, the Dominican Republic, and out to the USS *Comfort*, the Navy's flagship floating hospital. Destroyers tried to maintain a 10-mile exclusion zone around the carrier. On January 16 President Obama signed Executive Order 13529, calling up military and USCG reserves to support Operation Unified Response.

Over the relief phase of Operation Unified Response, JTF-Haiti evacuated between 13,000 and 16,000 American citizens, helicoptered 343 patients, flew 3,300 sorties, provided 2.6 million liters of fresh water, 17 million pounds of food, performed 1,000 medical surgeries, and treated up to 19,000 patients. U.S. Navy Seabees reopened docks at Port-au-Prince to shipping by January 20th; eventually 8,000 shipping containers and over 13 million tons of relief supplies would be brought ashore. Over 2,000 structures were assessed for damage, and shelters were provided for 525,000 displaced families (Ryan 2010, 9; Cecchine et al 2013).

The effectiveness of the JTF-Haiti effort was the result of shear numbers of forces, what military strategists refer to as mass, or concentration of force; some efficiency was lost in the process. The verbal ordering of forces at the outset (VOCOs) resulted in "responders arriving without the situational awareness and direction that a more conventional, condition-

---

[74] Author's interview with a member of USAF 21st STS, 2014.

[75] "Mishap" is a military term for aircraft accident or fatal crash.

based planning approach would have provided" (Cecchine et al 2013). Like the inevitable bottlenecks and missteps that occur in the fog of war, humanitarian assistance and disaster response operations presented their own challenges, akin to the old adage about the invalidity of war planning once the first bullet is fired. For example, there were limits on the number of patients that the military could treat, needs for MEDEVAC flights far exceeded the available number of helicopters, and medical prioritization of mission needs conflicted with other helicopter mission priorities because there was no mechanism for field assessment, nor a tracking system for the numerous, and incomplete MEDEVAC requests (Clementson 2011, 29-30).

Communications were also challenging. General Keen had started with a Blackberry and a single phone line and the use of Ambassador Merton's long-distance calling card; now the JTF was bringing in sophisticated communications gear from units around the globe, but it wasn't all compatible:

> The JCSE [Joint Communications Support Element] aided communications with the Deployable Joint Command and Control (DJC2) suite, which provided access to about 200 workstations, as well as other "workarounds." Providing communications, however, was complicated by two factors. A site not subject to flooding and suitable for construction of a platform had to be located, and DJC2 was incompatible with XVIII ABC ACP's [18th Airborne Corps Assault Command Post] Executive Communications set, which arrived on 17 January (Mandeles 2010, 26).

However, as the RAND report stated, "The speed that made Operation Unified Response successful
may have been obtained at some cost in efficiency and acceptance of risk, but those costs and risks were mitigated by the decisive leadership provided by the JTF-Haiti commander, LTG P. K. (Ken) Keen, and a serendipitous set of circumstances favoring the relief effort" (RAND 2013, xii).[76] RAND also stated that, "the rapid rush to get people and resources to the scene before any formal requirements assessment may have resulted in inefficiencies -- more of some resources than could be effectively used, and less than was needed of others" (RAND 2013, 40). Such is war and disaster.

FEMA: VA-TF1/USA-1, Port-au-Prince University

VA-TF1 had been working around the clock for a week, literally. Their commanders had organized the heavy and medium teams to sustain 24-hour operations, with one shift on during the day, and one at night; but many of them worked longer, conducting complicated technical rescues as they tunneled into the collapsed concrete structures. They had spent the first few days at the Hotel Montana looking for survivors. They had successfully rescued six people at the Montana and seen hundreds of fatalities. One of the people they looked for was a USAF Lieutenant Colonel; they didn't find him in the rubble.[77]

---

[76] RAND cited the serendipitous circumstances as General Keen's presence in Haiti and his relationship with General Floriano Peixoto, the survival of the communications infrastructure at the U.S. Embassy in Haiti, and the readiness of key U.S. Army units to deploy (RAND 2013, xii).

[77] Lieutenant Colonel Ken Bourland's body was recovered from the Hotel Montana in February 2010 by the Army Corps of Engineers, nearly a month after he was killed in the earthquake (Ruisi 2010).

The team had shifted its rescue work to Port-au-Prince University, where a four-story dormitory building had collapsed in what they called a "pancake" collapse. As a VA-TF1 member described it, the quake had shaken the earth laterally back and forth for about 45 seconds, followed by a fast vertical drop of the Haitian earth as the tectonic plates shifted against each other. During the shaking, hundreds of students had fled down the stairwell of the building in an escape attempt, which was stopped when the earth dropped, causing all four floors of the building to collapse on one another.[78] While many of the students were crushed, there were some void spaces in the concrete rubble, and some survivors. VA-TF1 was in the process of pulling one survivor out after a 26-hour straight rescue attempt to tunnel to reach her. A 27-year old student, she was severely injured; the team's medical staff intubated her, providing a breathing tube down her throat. One of her legs was crushed and pinned under the concrete rubble, and the team's doctors performed a field amputation of her leg at the femur to free her.

International protocol dictates that rescue teams turn survivors over to local health authorities, and VA-TF1 had kept to the rules for the other survivors that they had rescued over this week. But this woman would not have survived in the local care of Haitian medical providers. They did not have the medical facilities to save her. There was an Air Force field hospital for Americans that had been flown in and set up at the airport; they turned to their USAF pararescue team partners, who had been with them all week for security. The task force doctor and the pararescuers loaded the girl into their Humvee and sped to the airport. At first, the medical staff resisted treating the Haitian girl, but the pararescue airmen insisted. One stated, "I'll have my ass chewed but I'm not letting that girl die." The Air Force medical staff assumed care for the girl and she was eventually transferred to a hospital in Milot, Haiti.[79]

"Those guys put their careers on the line," Battalion Chief Stanley would say later. She added, "We were able to save so many lives because we got notified so fast."[80]

Back at the embassy, the IMAT personnel and FEMA staff were doing the best they could to support the effort, without feeling the same direct satisfaction of the US&R team members. By the fourth or fifth day on the ground, they were still "shopping" for work; trying to integrate into the embassy's workflow. It was frustrating for a team who basic mission is to organize chaos. They were becoming familiar with the embassy culture and building trust; however, some of their best staging and logistics personnel were assigned to help process new passports for American citizens seeking to be repatriated, essentially wasting their expertise. Nevertheless, they set up lines and processes at the airfield, processing thousands of U.S. citizens. They also supported the distribution of food and water; "we had MREs, but needed beans and rice," said one FEMA leader.[81] They took on an effort to design a system to care for infants, and they worked with the Navy to get the piers back open at the port. Here the DOG's Coast Guard admiral proved very helpful. They tried to help with any job they could. One IMAT member's first assignment was in the form of a name and a number handed to her on a yellow post-it note: an NGO needed fuel. The DART team "didn't want anything to do with them." FEMA offered to help. Using her

---

[78] Author's interview with a member of VA-TF1, 2014. The World Trade Center (WTC) buildings collapse on 9/11/2001 is a widely seen example of a pancake collapse. There were also some survivors in the stairwells in the WTC.

[79] Author's interview with FEMA personnel, 2014.

[80] Ibid.

[81] Author's interview with a senior FEMA official, 2013. "MREs" are meals ready-to-eat, the prepackaged food designed for the high calorie intake of soldiers, and stockpiled by FEMA for immediate disaster distribution.

satellite phone, the team member used a professional contact in a FEMA region in the U.S. to verify that the NGO was legitimate. The next day, she was able to arrange fuel for the NGO; it turned out that they were feeding thousands of people. The NGO became a partner, and Damon Penn made her the "Crisis Intervention Manager", which meant all the random post-it notes came to her. After two weeks, she was placed on a "committee for unaccompanied children" by the USAID team, the first time they were asked to be involved with USAID's functions.[82]

Within two to three weeks, the embassy was achieving a operational "battle rhythm", the expression used for the tempo that develops with an established daily routine in military command posts. The IMAT personnel worked for two weeks until they were demobilized. The rest of the FEMA staff and IRT members would depart in staccato bursts. Stated one team member, "None of the things we did were what we normally do. Persistence is what you needed in Haiti. Make order out of chaos, even in the smallest of ways."[83]

---

[82] Author's interview with IMAT member, 2014.
[83] Ibid.

CHAPTER V. OBSERVATIONS & FINDINGS

This section details the observations and finding of this research, including observations on how the DROs matched the Disaster Response Center (DRC) and Harrald typologies, observations regarding the specific independent and dependent variables, and a discussion of alternative explanations. Findings regarding the impact of paramilitary cultures on how organizations sped into action in response to the Haiti earthquake and concluding thoughts on this research are also presented.

OBSERVATIONS

The response to the earthquake in Haiti provides several observations related to disaster response organizations and paramilitary professional cultures.

Organizational Archetypes

Using the Disaster Response Center (DRC) typology of disaster responses, all the response types were present: the USCG cutter and aviation response could be considered a Type I (*established*) organization: they responded and performed diverse missions within the USCG mission portfolio. As one of their officers stated, the provision of situational assessments, rescue and medial operations, power, food, and water are something they do everyday; this was just on a bigger scale.[84]

Both FEMA and SOUTHCOM are harder to characterize within this typology, exhibiting different characteristics as the incident progressed. SOUTHCOM started out as a Type I (*established*) organization, but was forced to develop a different organizational structure in the middle of the incident to deal with the routine processing of military resources and orders, becoming a Type II (*expanding*) response organization.[85] Joint Task Force-Haiti was a newly established structure, designed to deal with the novel events of the earthquake, and represents a Type IV (*emergent*) response organization. Similarly, FEMA's responding assets were forced to perform both regular (rescue) and non-regular functions, notably the deployment of its teams internationally. FEMA's Incident Management Assistance Teams (IMAT) reflected a Type III (extending) response organization, performing non-regular tasks with its traditional organization. As one IMAT member stated, "nothing we did was routine." FEMA's Urban Search and Rescue (US&R) teams operated in non-traditional, ad hoc organizational structures under the international system to carry out rescues; at times merging their various rescue teams and creating cross function teams of medical, rescue, and search specialists, and blending in with Air Force pararescuers. The FEMA US&R team represents Type II (*expanding*) response teams. Figure 11 illustrates the placement of each of these organizations in the DRC typology. This analysis reveals that the 40-year old DRC typology, which predates FEMA, may be too simple a characterization for

---

[84] Author's interview with a Coast Guard officer, 2013.

[85] One might argue that because SOUTHCOM went from its novel 2008 organizational structure to a traditional (old) military J-code structure in the middle of the response, that it actually went from a Type II to a Type I organization. The important fact is that it was moved along this continuum between Type I and II, related to performing routine tasks.

some of our DROs, or it may only be able to capture snapshot of an organization at a particular point in time; nevertheless, it does provide a way to reflect on both the structure and the task of organizations in responding to a crisis.

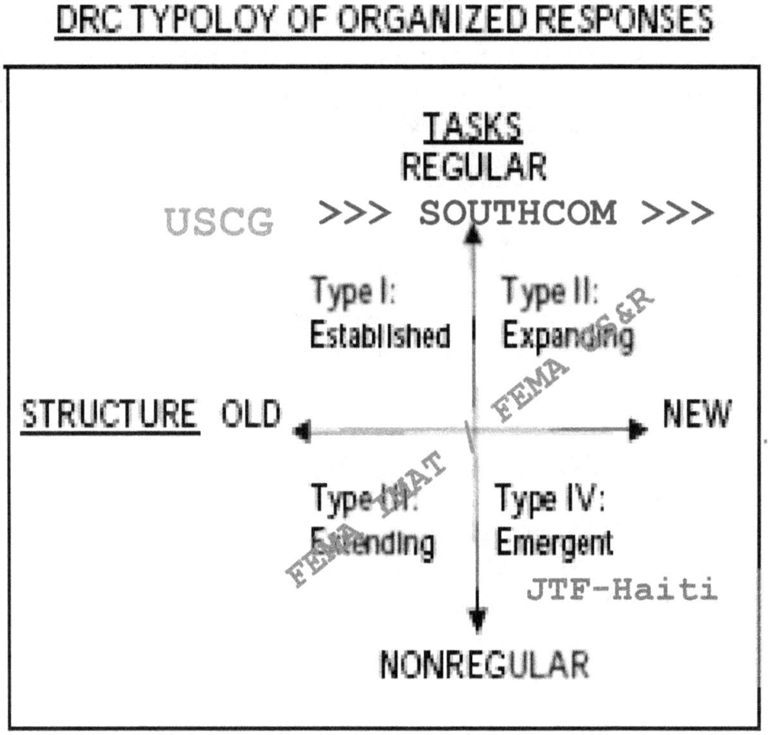

Figure 11. DRC TYPOLOGY OF SOME HAITI RESPONSE ORGANIZATIONS (Rodriguez et al 2007).

Similarly, using Harrald's typology, the USCG illustrated an agile and disciplined culture indicative of a *balanced/adaptive* response organization. SOUTHCOM used well-defined structures and processes to order up troops, but its rigid culture required the adoption of a traditional military J-code organizational structure. It fits best in the *bureaucratic/procedural* typology. JTF-Haiti was stood up in a rapid, ad hoc fashion, displaying creative thinking and improvisation to link multiple units together into a joint command: for example, deploying the 18th Airborne Corps Corp Assault Command Post to serve as staff, and calling in USAF special tactical squadrons to re-establish air traffic control. It appears that the throughout the organizational chain of command, the more designated a unit was for "special operations", the more capability for creativity and adaptability it displayed. As the incident progresses, however, routine processes were put into place, the more rigid and traditional the JTF-Haiti organization behaved. It therefore displayed *ad hoc/reactive* characteristics in the first two weeks of response, and then became much more *bureaucratic/procedural*.

FEMA is the hardest to characterize in this typology. Some of its response units displayed creativity -- the ability to take domestic teams and respond internationally with different team structures, or the improvisation displayed by its IMAT personnel in working in an entrepreneurial fashion to find productive contributions to the effort come to mind. On the other hand, some of its rigid processes were displayed as the response effort was mounted: the initial and immediate thought that, "we don't do international" comes to mind, as well as the cobbled-together efforts to secure transportation for the US&R and IMAT teams into Haiti. Figure 12 shows how these DROs fit into the Harrald typology.

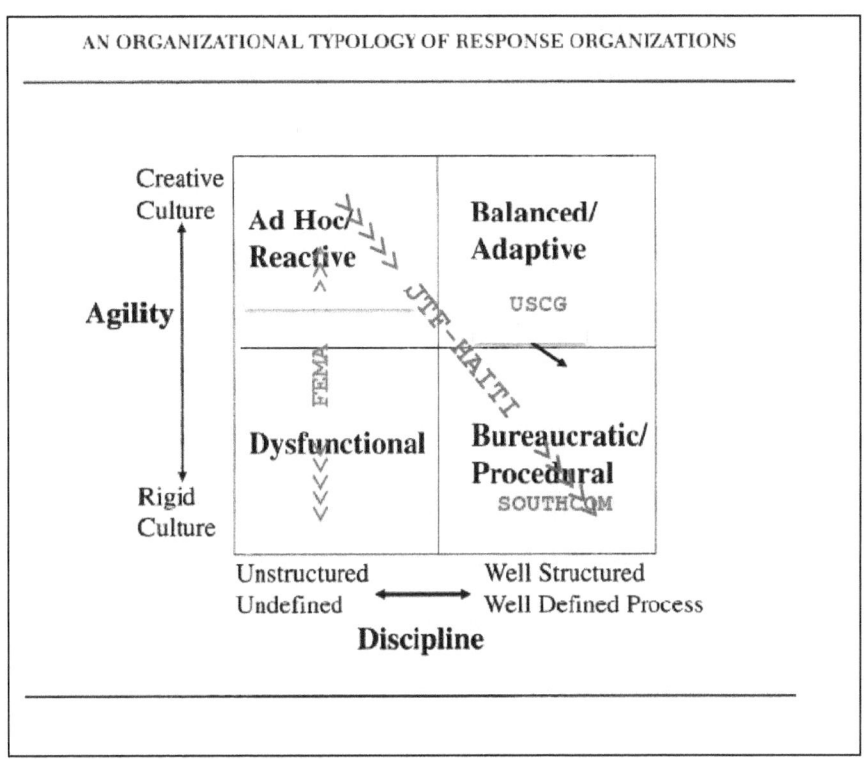

Figure 12. HARRALD'S TYPOLOGY OF DISASTER RESPONSE ORGANIZATIONS AS APPIED IN THE HAITI RESPONSE (Harrald 2006).

Haiti as Crisis

Haiti wasn't just an emergency, it was a crisis, fitting the crisis framework proposed by Leonard and Howitt; for the responders, the early days of the Haitian earthquake presented aspects of a crisis emergency. There was *low awareness* of the massive scale of the earthquake, compounded by the destruction of the Haitian government and the deaths of many of the United Nations staff that been based there. A U.S. military after action report listed the "unknowns" for the response: "migrant operations, security situation, lead federal agency requirements, available resources, JTF headquarters, MINUSTAH status, U.N. status, host government status, rules of engagement and logistics and maneuver requirements" (Operation Unified Response 2010, 15). Overcoming these unknowns, as well as responding and acting in spite of them, would take days and weeks.

For the United States, there was a *lack of a comprehensive script* for dealing with a humanitarian overseas emergency in the American sphere of influence inside another sovereign nation.[86] The U.S. *customized and improvised* the response to meet survivor needs, for example, for the first time FEMA deployed domestic Urban Search and Rescue (US&R) teams overseas to supplement its two American USAID international rescue teams.[87] *Tolerance of fault* in response efforts within the national of Haiti were hard to assess, but to some degree, in the short run, the Haitian citizens and the U.S. media understood this was an event of such as magnitude that it could not be easily fixed; in the week after the earthquake, the New York Times editorial board wrote, "An earthquake this size would have been a catastrophe in any country. But this was only partly a natural disaster. Look at Haiti and you will see what generations of misrule, poverty and political strife will do to a country" (Editorial 2010).

There was no single agency that had *specified skills* to bring to the problem, leading the President to call for a "whole of government" approach and designating USAID administrator Rajiv Shah (newly sworn in as head of USAID only days earlier) as the lead "coordinator" for the U.S. government (Operation Unified Response 2010, 101). As another example, both FEMA's administrator Craig Fugate and USCG Commandant Thad Allen assisted the USAID administrator at USAID's ad hoc command post in Washington. This had not occurred in the past. Allen and Fugate also placed a FEMA MERS communications vehicle and team aboard a USCG C-130 and flew it to Port-au-Prince, to provide robust communications capability at the embassy. The previously mentioned FEMA National Response Coordination Center (NRCC), used normally for domestic crisis management, was actually used as the ad hoc U.S. government coordination center for USAID; during interagency video conferences, FEMA employees actually removed the FEMA logos from the walls of the NRCC and replaced them with USAID logos.[88] Figure 13 illustrates this "whole of government" approach (Guha-Sapir et al 2011, 35).

---

[86] Haiti's earthquake response has resulted in an emerging effort to build an "international response framework" analogous to the *National Response Framework* (Analytic Services 2014).

[87] Only two USAID-sponsored urban search and rescue (US&R) teams are certified by the U.N. for international disaster response. FEMA has 28 teams with nearly identical training and equipment (and the two USAID teams are also FEMA teams). Therefore, this was a case of the U.S. deploying assets outside of the norm. While there were successes in the deployment of these FEMA teams, there were some problems in integrating them into international operations and supplying them with equipment (Lofton 2010).

[88] Interview with senior FEMA official, December 11, 2013.

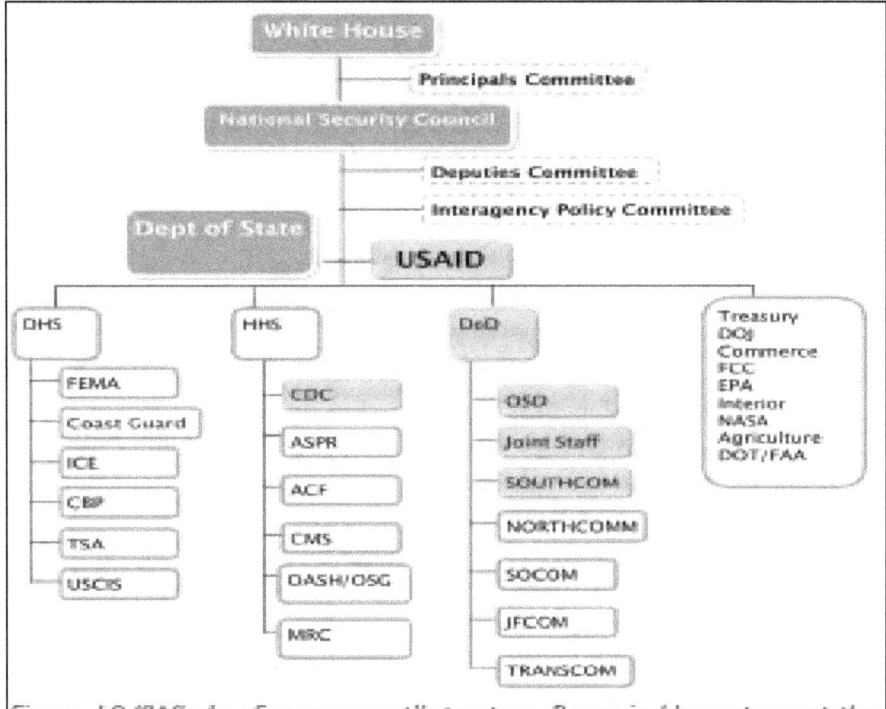

Figure 10: "Whole of government" structure. Boxes in blue represent the key offices within the US Government that set the policy guidance and strategic direction of the response: the White House, National Security Council, and Department of State. Boxes in orange represent the federal agencies that normally lead the USG international disaster response.

Figure 13. U.S. "WHOLE OF GOVERNMENT" RESPONSE TO THE HAITI EARTHQUAKE (Guha-Sapir et al 2011, 35).

A muted, more *collaborative command presence* was evident in the several command structures that were cobbled together in an ad hoc fashion, from the improvisational development of a coordinating body at the USAID headquarters in Washington, to the development of several military joint task forces (JTF) under the Department of Defense, to the use of the U.N. cluster system, to the maintenance of Haitian President Préval as the leader (in symbol if not reality).[89]

Cognitive-driven decisions became evident in the development of operational plans and the transition to the United Nation's relief effort. A *flattened organizational structure* was used during the incident by SOUTHCOM as it transitioned to its flatter, traditional J-code structure.

INDEPENDENT VARIABLES

Career Ladders: Insider or Outsider?

The DROs in Haiti had different career ladders. The USCG and SOUTHCOM have an insider career ladder, reflective of a career military organization. This career ladder is

---

[89] In addition to JTF-Haiti, SOUTHCOM established a JTF-Migration in case of illegal migration of refugees, and a JTF-Logistics to handle the long term movement of aid into the country.

characterized by personnel who are recruited at the entry level of the organization, and then receive professional development, training, and education as they move up through the organization's leadership rungs. Each subsequent assignment builds both individual and collective experience in the organization. The entry-level experiences are especially relevant because they contain an indoctrination period, which is considered a boot camp and officer training program in the military.

The insider career track appears to have had a positive effect on the speed at which these military organizations were able to respond. In the case of SOUTHCOM, General Keen had a professional relationship with Major General Floriano Peixoto Vieira Neto of Brazil, the commander of the U.N. MINUSTAH forces; this relationship had been forged during a specific foreign exchange program during Keen's professional development. Additionally, Keen had a friendship with Lieutenant General Frank Helmick, commander of the 18th Airborne Corps at Fort Bragg, who send his Assault Command Post (ACP) and top staff to support the creation of JTF-Haiti (Ryan 2010, 6). Both these relationships were a direct result of an insider career ladder that helped forge networks between these men. The importance of networks for effective disaster management has previously been explored in literature (see Rodriguez et al, and others) and it may be worth further study to explore if the relationship between an insider career ladder and speed is specifically related to this professional network or if networks become an intervening variable (i.e., is it "insider promotes speed" or "insider promotes network which promotes speed") (Rodriguez et al 2007). Whatever the relationship, as one retired coast guard admiral stated about his peers, "We've known each other for 30 years."[90]

FEMA, on the other hand, has an outsider orientation. Staffers in FEMA are hired at every level, from entry-level employee to the FEMA administrator. Only in the past year has an effort been made to develop a short indoctrination program for new employees who are mentored by a member of FEMA's Senior Executive Service, and personnel have very limited, non-integrated professional development opportunities.[91] As one senior FEMA official stated, "In 30 years of the military, I spent 5 years in training. We [FEMA] send people to school for a week and think they are managers."[92] Did this "outsider" career ladder slow FEMA down in responding to Haiti? The answer is a bit murky. Compared to the USCG and SOUTHCOM, FEMA personnel certainly have fewer 30-year relationships, and less opportunity for sustained professional development that increases the institutional experience of the agency as a whole. Another explanation may be that the insider career ladder functions to further embed and institutionalize cultural experiences in organization members, binding them together (as in Edgar Schein's culture definition), and that outsider organizations don't have the this same benefit for building the culture (Schein 2004). So while it seems that an insider career ladder might support organizational speed into action, it also may be that this comes from an integrated and networked culture, arising from people working together for many years. So an alternate explanation may be that experience (defined as cumulative time people in the organization have worked together) might lend itself to speed, as compared to outsider career ladders, where they have not worked together for very long.

It seems that there is a connection between an insider career ladder and speed, whether that is the result of professional development, networks, or experiences of people

---

[90] Author's interview with a USCG officer, 2013.

[91] Author's interview with a senior FEMA official, 2014.

[92] Author's interview with a senior FEMA official, 2013.

having worked together. Lack of time working together, a result of this outside career ladder orientation, may be why one FEMA official stated that, "FEMA is good at pick-up games"; and also why former FEMA Deputy Administrator Richard Serino is reported to have stated during the Hurricane Sandy response, "Can't we at least look like we have done this before?"[93]

Paramilitarism

Paramilitarism, what Langston has defined as aspects of military culture, but are "not designed for the sole purpose of violence," are embedded to some degree in each of the DROs in Haiti (Langston 2000).

Certainly, we have the career military professionals that made up SOUTHCOM and JTF-Haiti. They have been through the previously ascribed boot camps, wear uniforms, maintain a hierarchy and chain of command, and have certain rituals and ceremonies that are maintained to highlight significant personal or organizational milestones. By definition, SOUTHCOM and JTF-Haiti maintain a "thick" paramilitary culture. Did this impact their speed into action in Haiti in a positive way? The answer seems to be both yes and no. In some ways, the thick culture slowed response: SOUTHCOM's surge staff from other military directorates were unable to adapt to its organizational structure, for example, and it was forced to reorganize itself during the first week of the response. Clear mission orders are paramount for military personnel, and it seems that the clear, pre-established mission of enforcing anti-migration efforts led SOUTHCOM to send its only available and trained JTF command and control unit to set up JTF-Migration in Guantanamo Bay, rather then deploy them to the uncertain mission in Haiti. This forced General Keen and his staff to cobble together various units to form JTF-Haiti in Port-au-Prince. As a senior official stated, "paramilitary is not a start-up culture"; paramilitary organizations like having pre-set and detailed plans in place, and orderly execution of orders.[94] Military cultures also tend to bring a security mindset, as was illustrated by Nagl and Young in discussions of HA/DR response; in this case the focus on security may have delayed deployment of U.S. Health and Human Services (HHS) Deployable Medical Assistance Teams (DMAT) while they where told to wait for security at the Port-au-Prince airport (Nagl and Young 2000).[95] It certainly explains the diversion of the only SOUTHCOM JTF command unit to Guantanamo Bay in case of migrant problems.

The military's readiness for response and modular "plug-n-play" organizational units and chain of command is designed to facilitate speed into action. As one officer explained, "In the military, personnel know their peers, know the organizational language and lexicon, and divide and conquer problems. People know their roles and there is no arguing when crews are told what to do."[96] Its not a pick-up game, but requires training, experience and teamwork. However, this appears confined to military-to-military integration, and there is more difficulty with military-to-civilian integration. As one former member of the USCG described, the military has difficulty with the civilian incident command system (used

---

[93] Interviews with senior FEMA officials, 2013-2014.

[94] An earlier example of this are some less known but limited critiques of the 82nd airborne response to Hurricane Katrina in New Orleans; some felt their arrival was delayed for 48 hours because the entire force was mustered together, rather than deploying units piecemeal as they were ready. Author's conversation with Professor Dutch Leonard, 2008.

[95] Interview with a FEMA official, 2014.

[96] Author's interview with a USCG officer, 2014.

domestically across the U.S.) being independent from rank.[97] In the case of Haiti, while SOUTHCOM and JTF-Haiti were able to coordinate among various military forces in a joint effort, to included U.N. MINUSTAH forces, the integration with civilian humanitarian response organizations took longer. As an example, JTF-Haiti had to invent its Humanitarian Assistance Coordination Center (HACC) to serve as an integrating organizational element with the humanitarian organizations and U.N. cluster system.

In other cases, the military culture did support speed, and exhibited it with great effect. The greatest example might be the deployment of the USAF special tactics squadron, landing overnight and setting up air traffic control operations with 26 hours of the earthquake. But even they had to improvise to obtain an aircraft and work up through the military chain of command to deploy. It may be that Special Forces units have an ingrained ability to overcome some of the cumbersome military deployment processes and procedures.

FEMA serves an example of a DRO with a "thin" paramilitary culture. It doesn't have many ceremonies or traditions among its personnel, all of whom are civilian. The closest example of a paramilitary organization within FEMA may be its US&R teams, which have clear command hierarchies and division of labor, protective equipment which serves as uniforms; while US&R teams are partially funded by FEMA, however, they are actually made up of local government first responders, chiefly firefighters and paramedics. But the rest of FEMA is essentially a civilian workforce. Its organizational culture was described as much more heterogeneous and fragmented than the military, despite some older, former military desk officers in its ranks. As one former FEMA official noted, "FEMA has no sense of history, no positive projection of past, therefore no idea of its future. There is no culture of celebration of success in FEMA."[98]

One FEMA official stated that while the headquarters response directorate has some paramilitary artifacts, such as the NRCC and some deployable teams and components, it is much less present in FEMA regions, and negligible in directorates like those that handle its grants programs.[99] In the case of FEMA, this may have impacted its ability to recognize, respond, organize and act. In some cases, FEMA personnel discounted the earthquake reports, because, as one said, "We don't do international." In other cases, staff had to be deployed in an ad hoc fashion, bring its IMAT-West personnel from decentralized locations, sending senior staff from FEMA headquarters and the White House to figure out what was occurring, and even simply getting fuzzy orders to "figure it out when they get there." There was a lot of good done by its deployed personnel, but they lacked the modular ability of the military to link together; even the US&R teams had to improvise command structures to oversee its multiple operations in a new way. IMAT staff had to act in an entrepreneurial fashion, working to gain the trust of embassy staff and humanitarian partners alike. For example, Assistant FEMA Administrator Penn's authority was great enhanced after several days when embassy staff realized that a two-star admiral was reporting to him. In spite of this, it could be argued that the thin paramilitary culture within FEMA didn't play much of a role in the overall speed of recognition or response of the crisis, but it does appear to have

---

[97] Author's interview with a retired Coast Guard chief. ICS positions are filled based upon qualification, not rank. It is common for a senior officer to report to a junior officer during the temporary ICS structures that dominate domestic emergency response.

[98] Author's interview with a former senior FEMA official, 2013.

[99] Author's interview with a former senior FEMA official, 2014.

had some impact on the ability to organize its response personnel and integrate them into the international operation.

Somewhere in between the thick culture of SOUTHCOM and JTF-Haiti and the thin culture of FEMA sits the USCG. While its members are proud to declare themselves a military force, and they have thick cultural symbols and artifacts that date to their founding in 1789, the USCG also has non-military missions, from search and rescue operations, to safety and navigation of waterways. Its personnel operate in a joint environment with civilian counterparts on many routine day-to-day activities and it uses the civilian incident command system in responding to hazardous materials spills, while at the same time embedding its officers in military "joint" combat commands like SOUTHCOM around the world. As Commandant Thad Allen has said, the USCG is inherently "bureaucratically multilingual" and able to bridge the gap between these the military and civilian worlds.

Unlike FEMA, the USCG has a clear sense of its history and culture, its headquarters has pictures of past USCG leaders depicted in a "rogues gallery"; and it celebrates the actions of past members, helping build on its cultural bias towards action: as another retired officer stated, in the USCG, "there is always a ship named the Munro" (Douglas Munro is the USCG's only Medal of Honor recipient, earned in World War 2).[100] It has a thick culture, but one embedded in action; hence the preparation of the USCGC *Forward* prior to receiving orders to deploy from Guantanamo Bay, its ability to quickly link up with Haitian Coast Guard members and organize other USCG vessels and air traffic control (until relieved by the USAF special operations personnel), and then move quickly on to assessing roadways and ports and providing water, food, and medical treatment to the injured in rapid succession.

Workforce Autonomy

The ability to make autonomous decisions is a cornerstone of the Friedson characteristic of a profession, unlike managerially controlled bureaucratic work or customer driven tradecraft (Friedson 1986, Friedson 2001). This research on Haiti's earthquake provides examples of two units that exhibited this sort of professional autonomy: the U.S. Coast Guard and the U.S. Air Force's Special Tactics Squadron.

The USCG builds an organization in which leaders are taught to exhibit autonomous leadership from very early in their careers. They assume command of independent ships far earlier than their peers in the U.S. Navy. Many also become pilots of aircraft and helicopters that operate on independent search and rescue (SAR) missions, unlike Navy and Air Force aircraft that operate as part of squadrons. As one retired USCG admiral stated, "At every level I was empowered to do the job, to be accountable, but to take risks."[101]

The willingness to take on risk seems closely related to this professional autonomy. Several officers stated that the USCG has a high tolerance of risk and a culture that is forgiving of mistakes. As another officer stated, "Its your aircraft, you call the shots." When this acceptance of risk is supported by doctrine and policy (like USCG *Pub 1*), a history of independent action that is celebrated (the story of Douglas Munro), and is combined with professional training and education and career experiences that places leaders

---

[100] Author's interview with a USCG officer, 2013. Douglas Munro is the USCG's only Medal of Honor recipient, earned posthumously for actions in the saving of U.S. Marines on Guadalcanal in World War 2, http://www.uscg.mil/history/people/MunroDouglasIndex.asp.

[101] Author's interview with a retired USCG officer, 2013.

in positions of high autonomy ("its your aircraft"), an organizational bias towards action seems inevitable.

FEMA seems to be the opposite of the USCG in allowing autonomous action, although it has been trying to rebuild its workforce and its organizational doctrine and training since the low point of Hurricane Katrina. Several current and former FEMA officials described the organization as one that exhibits a persistent struggle between burdensome policies and processes (many imposed domestically by the legal interpretations of the Stafford Act) and some entrepreneurial personnel who seek creative ways to work around issues to solve problems. One FEMA official stated that FEMA is not good at routines and processes, but its a great place for "open field running", meaning that if personnel can get clear of the regulations and processes, they can make great progress.[102]

In Haiti, FEMA personnel were both limited by bureaucratic processes and worked to overcome them. The IMAT team, for example, bumped into some issues in trying to integrate with USAID's DART team. They didn't speak the same lexicon, and there was organizational resistance on the part of the USAID personnel to a FEMA "takeover", so FEMA personnel did what they have become accustomed to doing -- they worked around the managerial processes and procedures to come up with creative ways of helping, whether it was getting fuel to an NGO or helping build an ad hoc tripartite committee of U.N., Haitian, and FEMA decision makers to help coordinate aid delivery, debris removal, or sheltering of survivors. As one former FEMA senior official stated, "we go after opportunities."[103] Some were able to find those opportunities, some were not, especially the logistics and resource staging personnel, who were underutilized and ended up assisting with processing American citizens for repatriation back to the U.S. mainland. At one point, FEMA was prevented from handling out its infamous blue tarps, "Our tarps weren't up to U.N. standards," according to the U.N., said a FEMA official.[104]

FEMA's history is one of punctuated failure: Hurricane Andrew, Hurricane Katrina. There is no "rogues gallery" of pictures of former FEMA leaders in its hallways.[105] As another former FEMA official stated, "FEMA's benchmark is failure."[106] It has therefore grown a risk adverse culture in which personnel have to find work-arounds and "open fields" in order to take action. Some of these limits on its workforce autonomy are self-imposed, and some are external, whether it be the limits in legal authorities from the Stafford Act or limits placed on it in Haiti by external agencies such as USAID or the U.N. One FEMA official stated that the best FEMA employees work creatively under the rules, attempting to apply novel solutions despite the bureaucracy; a contrast to the "rule-breaking" when necessary autonomy built into the Coast Guard's organizational DNA.

SOUTHCOM and JTF-Haiti also appear managerially-driven and bureaucratic. The military hierarchy and chain of command limit autonomy, although individual unit commanders can act within mission parameters. In Haiti, the most autonomous displays of activity were exhibited by the Air Force special operations units that re-established the air traffic control at the airport. It helped to have the Deputy Commander of SOUTHCOM,

---

[102] Interview with a senior FEMA official, 2014. "Open field running" is a football expression describing the speed of an offensive player to advance the ball once he gets past a group of defensive players and can sprint down the field.
[103] Interview with a senior FEMA official, 2014.
[104] Ibid.
[105] Interview with a senior FEMA official, 2013.
[106] Ibid.

General Keen, in the country calling for help; but the formal processes of EXORDs and other approvals were still needed to respond and act.

Only the military special operations units seem to have high autonomy. For example, the members of the USAF 21st STS are trained to operate behind enemy lines, where life and death decisions must be made without the benefit of time to get orders from higher up the chain of command. After improvising ATC operations at the airport, other STS pararescuers quickly attached themselves to VA-TF1's US&R team, providing transportation, security, and access to medical care for survivors.

Table 9 summarizes the findings of the research about each DRO's paramilitary cultural attributes.

Variables			
Paramilitarism *Thick or Thin*	Thick	Thick	Thin
Career Ladder *Insider or Outsider*	Insider	Insider	Outsider
Workforce Autonomy *High or Low Autonomy*	Low	High	Low

Table 9. PARAMILITARY CULTURAL ATTRIBUTES OF DROS.

DEPENDENT VARIABLE: SPEED INTO ACTION

Speed into action saved lives in Haiti. The USCG's and USAF's ability to quickly reopen Toussaint Louverture International Airport to relief flights; FEMA's rapid deployment of six US&R teams alongside the USAID teams; and the establishment of JTF-Haiti within 48 hours of the earthquake to handle the coordination of the large military operation, all helped bring to fruition President Obama's command for a whole of government approach.

It seems that aspects of paramilitary culture did impact this overall speed into action. While the earthquake was widely recognized, the organizations with a paramilitary culture had pre-established routines and procedures for acting on that recognition, and personnel who could proactively prepare for an investable response. General Keen was quick to call upon SOUTHCOM's forces from Port-au-Prince. Captain Diane Durham readied her ship the moment the earthquake occurred. Other organizations took a small amount of time to come around to their role in the disaster.

Response to the disaster favored autonomy: the USCG didn't have to wait for orders to divert its resources from patrols. FEMA's US&R teams were activated, but then had to deal with the bureaucracy of getting passports ready, something military forces don't require, for example.

Speed of organizing was fostered by the plug and play modular capabilities between military to military units, even between U.S. and foreign nations, such as the U.N. MINUSTAH forces. Organizing was also fostered through longstanding personal networks that had developed between responders, such as that between General Keen and General Piexoto; this suggests that the insider career ladder found in military organizations may promote speed. But organizing was also slowed in the challenging interface between military and civilian organizations, especially with the U.N. cluster system and JTF-Haiti, which required the creation of a special organization sub-unit, the HACC, to serve as a translator and coordinator.

Ultimately, speed to action was fostered by certain aspects of workforce autonomy that is not often equated with large military organizations, but is reflected in workforce autonomy exhibited in professional cultures. Military Special Forces and the U.S. Coast Guard have fostered this autonomy. It is interesting to note that the cultures of both these organizations give leaders the autonomy to break some rules without fear of severe career consequence. Perhaps one angle that could be further explored is the role of rules and rule-breaking in a disaster setting, especially since some definitions of disasters concern the breakdown of societal norms for a temporary period of time. Perhaps it is in those time periods when rule-breaking has certain advantages over rule-following.

In fact, there could be many other explanations that also influence speed in relation to paramilitary cultural attributes, specifically workforce autonomy, career ladders, and paramilitarism. Table 10 summarizes the observations of how these independent variables appear to have influenced the speed into action in response to the Haiti earthquake.

Variables	FASTER	SLOWER
Paramilitarism *Thick or Thin*	Thick	Thin
Career Ladder *Insider or Outsider*	Insider	Outsider
Workforce Autonomy *High or Low Autonomy*	High	Low

Table 10. OBSERVED INFLUENCE ON SPEED INTO ACTION.

Other Influences on Speed into Action

The actions of organizations often defy simple explanations, and there are other variables that may have also influenced the speed at which these DROs were able to recognize, respond, organize, and act. Some of these explanations were brought up by the interviewees.

One potential set of variables is in the make-up of the employee workforce. One interviewee, who had experience in two of the DROs that were researched, suggested that there could be a bias towards action in the employees hired into military organizations. This could have merit, as the military generally hires younger employees who may be seeking more action-oriented career roles.

Another key variable might be the sheer size of the organization, from small organizations to larger ones. FEMA is the smallest of the organizations observed here, with approximately 4,000 core employees and a total workforce of about 14,000 (inclusive of Disaster Response Corps and FEMA Corps members) (FEMA About 2014). The Coast Guard has about 50,000 personnel and another 40,000 reserves and auxiliary members. JTF-Haiti directed the operations of 22,000 military personnel (Cecchine et al 2013).

The stability of the workforce may also be a factor. SOUTHCOM has the benefit of career military officers, and while they do rotate through assignments every few years, the military chain of command is maintained. It has a fairly routine turnover, but one designed to maintain organizational stability. Likewise, the USCG also has a similar turnover as staff go through different assignments, and like SOUTHCOM, it is purposely designed to maintain organizational consistency. FEMA has had a high turnover of personnel, especially after it was merged into the Department of Homeland Security and then again after Hurricane Katrina; its IMATs are a relatively new organizational unit, mandated in the Post Katrina Emergency Management Reform Act (PKEMRA), but is US&R teams are consistent and relative personnel turnover is limited (Rubin 2012).

Other variables might also impact the speed at which these organizations recognize, respond, organize, and act after a catastrophe. For example, there may be a distinct difference in the type of workforce in each organization (e.g., full-time career staff in the U.S. Coast Guard, or the U.S. military's wide array of personnel, from full-time careerists, to reserves, to part-time National Guard, and DoD civilians). Alternately, whether leadership is careerist or politically appointed may have had an impact: FEMA has political appointees, the USCG and SOUTHCOM do not; the impact of political appointees has been studied in some of these organizations (Lewis 2008).[107]

Additionally, each agency might have different legal authorities that influence its speed; in the case of FEMA, for example, a senior official reported that the staff response in FEMA's National Response Coordination Center (NRCC) initially discounted the earthquake as relevant to FEMA, telling him minutes after the earthquake occurred, "we don't do international", a comment that could be interpreted from either a legal authority or an organizational culture perspective.[108]

---

[107] FEMA's part-time workforce has been undergoing transformation since the Haiti earthquake, transitioning from "Disaster Assistance Employees" to a "FEMA Reservist" program. The latter requires employees to maintain demonstrate proficiency through a formal set of job qualifications known as the FEMA Qualification System (FQS). Many Disaster Assistance Employees have been reluctant to "re-qualify" for positions for which they had previously been qualified, and have resigned.

[108] Author's interview with a senior FEMA official, December 12, 2013.

V. OBSERVATIONS & FINDINGS

These explanations have merit, and future research should try to take them into account. Organizations remain complicated entities and their behaviors can be viewed and explained in many ways.

FINDINGS

This work yields some overarching findings in relation to how these DROs were able to recognize, respond, organize, and act after the Haiti earthquake. This section discusses those overarching findings. Figure 14 visually depicts the process tracing method as a backdrop to these findings. As described earlier, process tracing is a qualitative method for case study analysis. It is built upon the work of George and Bennett, Brady, Mahoney, and Van Evera (George and Bennett 2005, Brady 2010, Mahoney 2010, Van Evera 1997). It focuses on both narrative description and sequential timing of events.

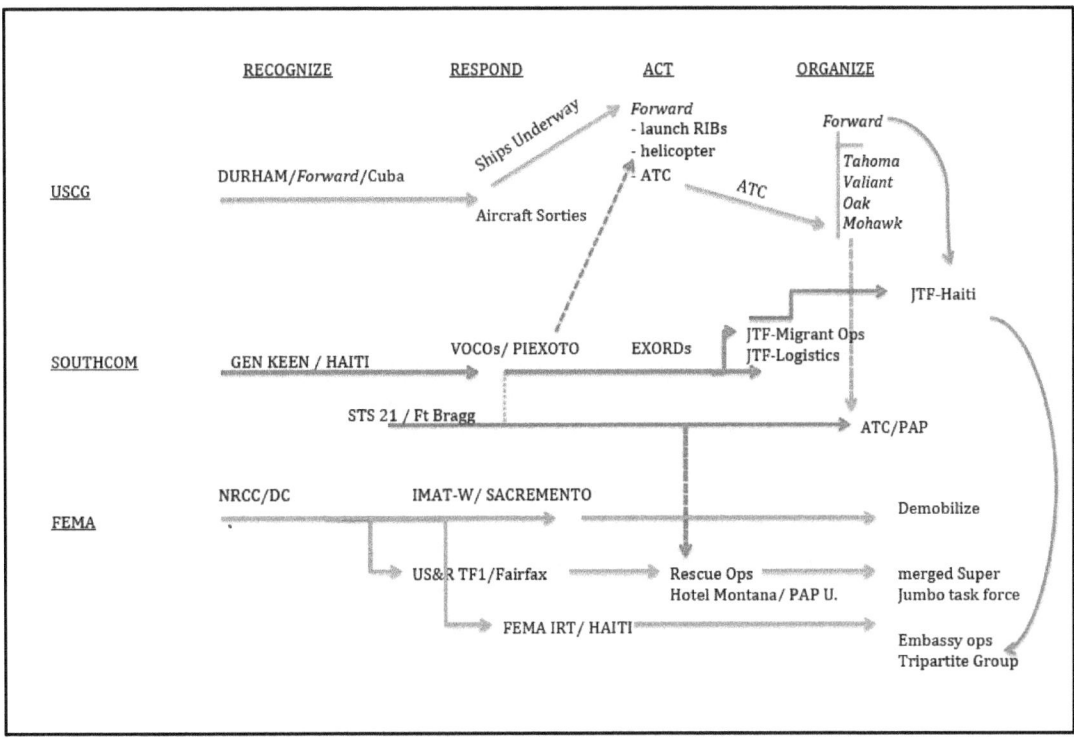

Figure 14. PROCESS TRACING OVERVIEW OF HAITI CASE

Acting Comes Before Organizing

One of the most evident findings is that there may be a flaw in the initial construct that was developed for speed, comprising the sequential steps of recognition, response, organization, and action. This research seems to support a sequence of recognition, response, *action*, then organization. In the case of FEMA, they responded and started doing some entrepreneurial humanitarian work and rescue efforts before figuring out how to fit into the USAID model; likewise, SOUTHCOM assets like the USAF's Special Tactics Squadron 21 began acting on mission-specific orders (i.e., reestablish ATC at the airport) before the orders to establish JTF-Haiti were issued by the Pentagon. USCGC *Forward* began flying assessment missions and providing aid with very limited orders from USCG District 7 in Miami and before the CTU was established.

In public administration, we celebrate the creation of effective and efficient managerial structures; these structures are inherent to the concept of administration; however, it may be that during a disaster, those effective and efficient structures are organized after the most important response actions are already underway. This is not accounted for in our response literature, doctrine, or training. Response doctrine, for example, focuses on the creation of incident management systems such as NIMS; and the military after action reports were critical of the speed at which units were deployed because it was disorderly. In the case of Haiti, acting came before organizing, and therefore speed into action comes at the expense of getting organized.

Autonomy Enables Speed

Another finding is that workforce autonomy appears to be a key driver of speed. The creation of professionals who are empowered to act under their own authority removes many of the managerial controls and barriers that are needed to authorize action. Thus, Commander Diane Durham could steam her ship for Haiti and engage in actions that she felt were most necessary, based on her knowledge, experience, and intuition.

On the other hand, organizations that need authorization to take action are slower. FEMA's deployed IMAT teams didn't know what they were authorized to do, nor how to integrate into the USAID processes and the U.N. cluster system. JTF-Haiti had to create processes to approve military operations in support of the humanitarian organizations.

FEMA effectively supported USAID despite unfamiliarity with process: "a lack of knowledge regarding either USAID or foreign disaster assistance mechanisms hampered response operations" according to their internal after action review (Lofton 2010, 25). FEMA needed permission from USAID before it could subtask other agencies: since it was not a Stafford Act incident, FEMA lacked its routine tasking authority (Lofton 2010, 26).

Insiders Career Ladders Help Build Personal Networks and Experiences, Which Facilitate Speed

In Haiti, "insider" career ladders facilitated professional and personal relations that promoted speed into action. The career development opportunities afforded to members of paramilitary organizations reviewed in this work had an impact on the speed of the disaster response. General Keen of SOUTHCOM had a personal and professional relationship with General Piexoto of MINUSTAH, allowing them both to quickly agree on role of each of their organizations within the first 24 hours of the disaster response. Likewise, General Keen's personal friendship with General Kendricks of the 18th Airborne Brigade at Fort Bragg led to quick deployment of Kendrick's Assault Command Post and staff, forming the nucleus of JTF-Haiti.

In a similar fashion the commander of the USCGC *Tahoma* had previously served in Haiti as a USCG liaison, and was assigned by Commander Diane Durham to reprise this role with the Haitian Coast Guard as the shore-based commander of USCG efforts.

Rule-breaking is Faster than Rule-following

In several cases, rule-breaking proved to be an enabler of speed to action. Commander Durham was forthright with her ship's rule-breaking in order to achieve speed, whether it was steaming without "lines down" overnight, entering the harbor without a harbor master, providing the *Forward*'s supplies and provisions to Haitian's, she and her crew improvised around or in spite of USCG rules and regulations. This rule-breaking was unofficially sanctioned and even celebrated in the USCG after the earthquake, based on after action discussions with her superior officers.[109]

---

[109] Author's interview with USCG officer, 2014.

General Keen's issuance of 16 pages of VOCOs (verbal orders of the commanding officer) promoted rapid military response by avoiding cumbersome request for forces (RFF) paperwork, even if it later became a problem for SOUTHCOM planners and logisticians (Cecchine et al 2013).

Likewise, USAF Special Tactics Squadron 21 worked around rules both to respond to the incident, by commandeering a USAF special operations C-130 that had been conducting routine training, managing up their chain of command for approval, by finding a way to work with the VA-TF1 US&R team, and later by ensuring that a Haitian student was treated by a USAF medical group that had set up at the airport to care for U.S. citizens.

Units that attempted to follow the rules were slower, and in some cases less successful. FEMA's IMAT personnel were de-mobilized after two weeks because they could not effectively find a way to work in the disorganized structures and lack of rules that existed in the international response environment.

Paramilitarism Speeds Organization

The facets of paramilitarism: hierarchy, modular structures, chains of command, and lines of authority help with the plug and play aspects of fitting ad hoc organizational pieces together. Traditional bureaucracy still has merits. Organizing is slower when there are not these paramilitary structures in place. As one interviewee stated, paramilitarism provides shared lexicon and clear understanding of roles and mission, unlike humanitarian organizations, which tend to have their own goals. Once SOUTHCOM reorganized into its J-structure, other military personnel could fit into its operations. Additional Coast Guard cutters fit under CDR Durham's command, and then in turn the Coast Guard operation was folding under the Navy's operations once the *Carl Vinson* arrived.

During the first weeks, the development of collective priorities and objectives in Haiti between civilian and military agencies was hard, as there was no organizing structure or authority until the tripartite group of the U.N., Haitian and U.S. government officials was established, and eventually a Haitian Government council was created in after the first few weeks.[110]

CONCLUDING THOUGHTS

The majority of the U.S. response to Haiti came from the military, coordinated through several of its combat commands. SOUTHCOM was the lead for coordinating military operations, after a specific determination that it would establish JTF–Haiti on the ground in Port-au-Prince, and a JTF-Migration Ops, made up of U.S. Army South (ARSOUTH) headquarters staff, in Guantanamo Bay, Cuba in the case of mass migration contingency operations.[111]

The "whole of government" response was not perfect. Several government agencies struggled in response to the quake. A case study on Haiti from the Joint Forces Staff

---

[110] Author's interview with senior U.S. government official, 2013.

[111] The author could find no record of coordination between JTF-Migrant Ops and a DHS structure set up in Florida to handle migration problems from the earthquake, the DHS Homeland Security Task Force South. Likely, both organizations (DoD and DHS) went to their own existing "playbooks" on-hand in the face of the uncertainty of the immediate crisis. But to paraphrase Donald Rumsfeld, absence of evidence is not evidence of absence [of communications between the two].

College reported on problems within USAID, the lead American agency charged with coordinating the response:

> Mobilization of USG [U.S. government] personnel was a major weakness. Leaders were unable to quickly tap into potential sources of personnel with disaster expertise and the lack of pre-response training and exercises significantly degraded the response. Expertise resident in the US State Department's Office for Reconstruction and Stabilization (S/CRS), for instance, were not employed due to an internal rift between USAID and S/CRS stemming from competing mission sets, budgetary considerations, and personalities. USAID-OFDA was not able to muster or hire additional staff to handle the magnitude of the crisis and pre-existing relationships were insufficient to augment staff from other agencies.[112]

U.S. government surge operations continued for 10 weeks. In total, the U.S. provided over 22,000 military personnel at the peak of the JTF-Haiti effort. In March 2010, the U.N. transitioned to long-term recovery.

Among the specific DROs researched here, FEMA, SOUTHCOM, and the USCG, one particular conclusion seems to stand out in comparison between these agencies: Haiti might have been a crisis for others, but for the USCG it was just another routine emergency.

The USCG proved it was extremely adept at achieving positive outcomes by partnering with others. Admiral Thad Allen has stated that incidents like Haiti pose a new challenge for public administration, one that will require a new synthesis between the Wilsonian dichotomy and the New Public Management's evolution towards citizen-centered, networked outcome processes: he sees the need for the involvement of a wide-array of nontraditional partners, transforming unity of command into unity of effort. Allen calls for leaders with political acumen and soft, boundary-spanning skills; he writes:

> Any response to a black swan event or wicked problem will involve public participation to a greater degree than any time in history. From the 24-hour news cycle to the role of nongovernmental organizations to the social media, the participation of the public is a permanent feature of the social ecology (Allen 2012).

As indicated from doctrine and validated by its senior officers, the USCG does seem to have at its core a competency of cooperation and partnership with others. Haiti illustrated this. The USCG was the first of many response agencies, in foreign waters and on foreign land. First responders like Commander Durham of the USCGC *Forward* had to be flexible, improvising a myriad of approaches to gain an understanding of what had occurred, where the most critical areas of need existed, and how to initiate actions with limited resources.

Interagency boundary-spanning efforts included coordination between the Department of State, USAID, the Department of Defense, the Department of Homeland

---

[112] DiOrio, David R. *Operation Unified Response: Haiti Earthquake 2010*, Joint Forces Staff College, 2010.

Security/FEMA, Haiti, the Dominican Republic, the United Nations, and a myriad of NGOs.[113] This was more difficult for other organizations.

The paucity of leadership from President Préval of Haiti, and the limited capability of USAID to coordinate a whole of government response, presented special challenges for the U.S. government. As the SOUTHCOM Commander, General Fraser, stated in his after action lessons report:

> From the start, the roles, responsibilities, authorities, and required capabilities of the lead federal agency were not clearly defined. While the designation as lead federal agency gave [USAID] broad authority to coordinate efforts, there was no specification of subordinate support relationships or division of labor. USAID had few personnel on the ground to form and lead the robust planning required early in the crisis (Keen et al 2010).

The international community response was also in disarray. The review of the United Nations response indicated that coordination and leadership were persistent challenges, since much of the local leadership had been killed or disrupted:

> …lack of local ownership, the humanitarian sector's difficulty in preparing for and responding to an urban disaster, as well as a weak assessment of the humanitarian situation and needs delayed the response and led to important gaps in geographical and sector-based coverage (Bhattacharjee and Lossio 2011).

As reported in the same after action report, it took the U.N. up to three weeks to make its cluster system functional, and inter-cluster organization remained weak.

Given the challenges faced by other experienced disaster response organizations to this international event, the USCG's ability to perform effectively stands in marked contrast. The multi-mission, maritime, military nature of the USCG -- combined with its culture of "figuring out how to achieve national outcomes in ambiguity and chaos" -- meant that its units were able to shift gears quickly into disaster roles without higher echelon approval, an example of high workforce autonomy.[114] With the right doctrine, professional development, and culture, paramilitary forces can handle complex humanitarian emergencies.

The USCG has developed a force that has managed to solve a challenge for other disaster response organizations, namely how to bridge the unique challenge of conducting disaster relief operations with a military force. This issue has been a specific problem for U.S. military forces in the past, which has not had a good history of managing the shift from security to disaster relief as Nagl and Young have described (Nagl and Young 2000).[115]

---

[113] While this paper indicates that these skills are culturally embedded within the USCG, they still may not be embedded in Coast Guard education to the satisfaction of its leadership. The USCG after action report from the Deepwater Horizon incident (occurring within the same timeframe as the Haiti incident) called for the establishment of an additional training course to address the specific need for new kinds of crisis education, focusing on leadership, decision-making, communications, and intergovernmental relations. (USCG *Deepwater Horizon ISPR Final Report* 2011.)

[114] Author's interview with a USCG Captain, 2013.

[115] For example, during Operation Restore Hope in Somalia, the Army units were "bewildered" by the overlap between warfighting and peacekeeping missions. See Nagl, John A. and Elizabeth O. Young. "Si Vis Pacem, Para Pacem: Training for Humanitarian Emergencies." *Military Review*, (2000).

V. OBSERVATIONS & FINDINGS

Prior experience with partnerships certainly helped the USCG. The USCG had also previously worked with U.S. military partners at SOUTHCOM on Caribbean exercises in 2009 (GAO 2010). USCG officers also spend much of their career interacting with diverse stakeholders and partners. Each port, for example, has a wide-array of private and public participants that the USCG officers must interact with regularly to achieve both their homeland security and non-homeland security missions.

In framing the earthquake within Leonard and Howitts' two disaster types (*routine* or *crisis*), while the Haitian earthquake may have been a crisis for many of the U.S. and international disaster response agencies, for the USCG, it seemed to be just another routine emergency (Leonard and Howitt 2007).

Other organizations struggled with low awareness (U.N. OCHA), lack of comprehensive scripts (The White House National Security Staff), improvised responses (USAID), incompletely specified skills (SOUTHCOM), collaborative command structures (U.N. cluster system), cognitive-driven decisions (U.S. military planners), and flattened organizational structure (SOUTHCOM).

However, the USCG seems to have approached the earthquake like any other mission. The USCG achieved high awareness (via aircraft grid surveys), used comprehensive scripts (based on its ICS training), displayed modest customization (by adapting the provision of power, water, medical, and communications to the incident), showed precision-execution (in the rapid deployment of aircraft and cutters), used well-defined and highly developed skills (like flying aircraft sorties), had leaders trained in the situation and how to respond (like Commander Durham), showed a command presence (the USCGC *Forward* was in harbor of Port-au-Prince the morning after the earthquake), used recognition-primed decision-making (in determining response priorities like establishing communications for the airfield and conducting air surveys without instruction), and displaying a hierarchical organization (through the command of its Captains at sea).

This research framework may provide useful if applied against other DROs, or in other disasters. For example, the Red Cross, USAID, and U.N. OCHA would make interesting organizations to study and expand this research. Humanitarian organizations tend to have an ethos that abhors paramilitary-like command and control, yet this research shows paramilitary culture did seem to play a role in the speed in which some DROs were able to recognize, respond, organize, and act.

For FEMA, this research seems to call for the development of a more robust, insider career ladder, one that will eventually lead to more workforce autonomy based on an indoctrinated, professional, and experienced staff. Through this process, FEMA may move beyond its bureaucratic culture. Emergency management must be more than professional, it must work to become more like Friedson's definition of a profession.

For the military, a continual effort to push autonomy down to lower echelon units and to build off its successful special operations culture may be a way to improve its humanitarian assistance and disaster response operations, especially in the face of non-routine, no-notice events that confound the normal military planning culture.

In contrast, it seems that the USCG was almost uniquely positioned among these responding agencies to navigate the complexities of the Haiti emergency response, certainly better than the U.N., USAID, and other U.S. military forces in its initial response. For the USCG, Haiti was just another emergency. Its thick level of paramilitarism, insider career ladder, and high workforce autonomy contributed to its speed into action. It was able to command, control, and coordinate. That is relevant for all disaster response organizations that seek to achieve effectiveness in large disasters.

V. OBSERVATIONS & FINDINGS

This particular case revealed that differences in organizational attributes like the level of paramilitarism, the degree of workforce autonomy, and an organization's career ladder did play some role in the speed at which three disaster response organizations were able to recognize, respond, act, and organize the provision of aid the victims of the Haiti earthquake. These specific variables (along with other potential influences on speed into action that were raised during this research) should be taken into consideration by both practitioners and academics as potential sources of variance in organizational performance, building upon the work of the Disaster Research Center, Harrald, Leonard and Howitt, and others, as we attempt to further our knowledge and understanding of organizations and disaster response.

THIS PAGE INTENTIONALLY BLANK

REFERENCES

Allen, Thad. "Confronting Complexity and Creating Unity of Effort: The Leadership Challenge for Public Administration." *Public Administration Revoew* 72, no. 3 (2012): 320-321.

American Red Cross. "American Red Cross Issues One-Month Progress Report for Haiti Earthquake." *Science Letter*, February 23 2010.

Analytic Services, Inc. *Coordinating the U.S. Response to Foreign Disasters: Concept and Considerations for a Framework.* Banyan Analytics, 2014.

Anderson, William A. *Facing Hazards and Disasters: Understanding Human Dimensions.* Washington, DC: National Research Council Committee on Disaster Research in the Social Sciences 2006.

Arjen Boin, Paul 'T Hart, Allan Mcconnell And Thomas Preston. "Leadership Style, Crisis Response and Blame Management: The Case of Hurricane Katrina." *Public Administration and Society* 88, no. 3 (2010): 706-723.

Barnard, Chester I. *The Functions of the Executive.* Cambridge, MA: Harvard University Press, 1938.

Bea, Keith. *Urban Search and Rescue Task Forces: Facts and Issues*, 2010.

Beas, Clayton C. and Brian K. Lysne. "Using a Model of Team Collaboration to Investigate Inter-Organizational Collaboration During the Relief Effort of the January 2010 Haiti Earthquake." Naval Postgraduate School, 2011.

Bennett, Andrew. 2010. "Process Tracing and Causal Inference." In *Rethinking Social Inquiry: Diverse Tools, Shared Standards*, 2nd ed., ed. Henry E. Brady and David Collier, 207–19. Lanham, MD. Rowman and Littlefield.

Bhattacharjee, Abhijit and Roberta Lossio. *Evaluation of OCHA Response to the Haiti Earthquake*, 2011.

Birdsall, Ian. "Looking for the FEMA Guy Part 1." *Administration & Society* 41, no. 4 (2009).

Birkland, Thomas A. *Lessons of Diaster: Policy Change after Catastrophic Events.* Washington, DC: Georgetown University Press, 2006.

Boin, Arjen and Cynthia Renaud. "Orchestrating Joint Sensemaking across Government Levels: Challenges and Requirements for Crisis Leadership." *Journal of Leadership Studies* 7, no. 3 (2013).

REFERENCES

Bowmen, Steve, Lawrence Kapp and Amy Belasco. *Hurricane Katrina: DoD Disaster Response*, Congressional Research Service 2006.

Brady, Henry E., David Collier, and Jason Seawright. "Refocusing the Discussion of Methodology." In *Rethinking Social Inquiry: Diverse Tools, Shared Standards*, 2nd ed., ed. Henry E. Brady and David Collier, 15–31. Lanham, MD: Rowman and Littlefield, 2010.

Braesch, Connie. "Guardians Report In: CDR Diane Durham." In *Coast Guard Compass: Offical Blog of the U.S. Coast Guard*, 2014, 2010.

Caldwell, Tom. "Military Support for FEMA USAR." In *Society of Military Engineers*. Fort Bragg, NC, 2013.

CALL. *Disaster Response Staff Officer's Handbook*, 2007.

Carley, Kathleen M. and John R. Harrald. "Organizational Learning under Fire: Theory and Practice." *American Behavioral Scientist* 40, no. 3 (1997): 310-332.

Cavallo, Eduardo, Andrew Powell and Oscar Becerra. "Estimating the Direct Economic Damages of the Earthquake in Haiti." *Economic Journal* 120, no. 546 (2010): F298-F312.

Cecchine, Gary, Forrest E. Morgan, Michael A. Wermuth, Timothy Jackson, Agnes Gereben Schaefer and Matthew Stafford. *The U.S. Military Response to the 2010 Haiti Earthquake: Considerations for Army Leaders* Santa Monica, CA: U.S. Army, 2013.

Chappell, Allison T. and Lonn Lanza-Kaduce. "Police Academy Socialization: Understanding the Lessons Learned in a Paramilitary-Bureaucratic Organization." *Journal of Contemporary Ethnography* 39, no. 1 (2010): 187-214.

Cheng, Cliff. "Uniform Change: An Ethnography on Organizational Symbolism, Volunteer Motivation and Dysfunctional Change in a Paramilitary Organization." *Leadership & Organization Development Journal* 19, no. 1 (1998): 22-31.

Christensen, Tom and Per Laegred. "The Whole-of-Government Approach to Public Sector Reform." *Public Administration Review* 67, no. 6 (2006): 1059-1066.

CIA, "The World Factbook" https://http://www.cia.gov/library/publications/the-world-factbook/geos/ha.html (accessed August 2013).

Clementson, Thomas and Charles Fisher. "Analysis of U.S. Military Helicopter Operations in Support of Humanitarian Assistance and Disaster Relief." Naval Postgraduate School, 2011.

Clifton, Nile L. *After Action Report, 01 June 2010 - 19 September 2010, Port Au Prince, Haiti*, 2010.

REFERENCES

CNN. 2005. "Mayor to Feds: 'Get Off Your Asses': Transcript of Radio Interview with New Orleans' Nagin," http://www.cnn.com/2005/US/09/02/nagin.transcript/ (accessed May 7, 2006).

Coffman, Edward M. *The Regulars: The American Army1898-1941*. Cambridge, MA: The Belknap Press, 2004.

Collier, David. "Understanding Process Tracing." *Political Science and Politics* 44, no. 4 (2011): 823-830.

Comfort, Louise. *Shared Risk: Complex Systems in Seismic Response*. First ed. Bingley, UK: Emerald Group Publishing Limited, 1999.

Congress. *Post Katrina Emergency Management Reform Act*, 2006.

Congress. *Robert T. Stafford Disaster Relief and Emergency Assistance Act, as Amended, and Related Authorities Pl 100-707*, 2007.

Creed, Patrick and Rick Newman. *Firefight: Inside the Battle to Save the Pentagon on 9/11*: Presidio Press, 2008.

Cross, American Red. "American Red Cross Details Haiti Earthquake Response and Plans for the Future." *Science Letter*, January 25 2011.

Cumming, William, Claire B. Rubin and Irmak Renda-Tanali. "Homeland Security Time Line: An Historical Overview of Civil Organizations (1933-2003)." Washington, DC, 2003.

DeBerry, Jarvis. "Lt. Gen. Russel Honore Showed Restraint New Orleans Police Did Not." *The Times-Picayune*, August 27, 2010.

Department of State, "Ambassador Kenneth Merton Biographical Information" http://zagreb.usembassy.gov/ambassador.html (accessed February 2014).

Devi, Sharmila. "Helping Earthquake-Hit Haiti." *The Lancet* 375, no. 9711 (2010): 267-8.

DiOrio, David R. *Operation Unified Response: Haiti Earthquake 2010*, 2010.

Dull, Matthew, Patrick S. Roberts, Michael S. Keeney and Choi Sang Ok. "Appointee Confirmation and Tenure: The Succession of U.S. Federal Agency Appointees, 1989-2009." *Public Administration Review* 72, no. 6 (2012): 902-913.

Editorial. "Haiti." *The New York Times*, January 14, 2010.

Evera, Stephen Van. *Guide to Methods for Students of Political Science*. Ithaca, NY: Cornell University Press, 1997.

REFERENCES

Farazmand, Ali, ed. *Handbook of Crisis and Emergency Management*. New York, NY: Marcel Dekker, Inc., 2001.

FEMA. *National Incident Management System*, 2008.

FEMA. *National Response Framework*, 2008.

FEMA. *The Federal Emergency Management Agency Publication 1*, 2010.

FEMA, "Release 101020: FEMA Administrator Craig Fugate Urges State Emergency Managers to Prepare for the Worst and Consider the Entire Community While Planning for Disaster" release 101020 (accessed January 22 2014).

FEMA. *A Whole Community Approach to Emergency Management: Principles, Themes, and Pathways for Action*, 2011.

FEMA. *Overview of Stafford Act Support to States*, 2012.

FEMA. *The State of FEMA*. Washington, DC, 2012.

FEMA. *Hurricane Sandy FEMA after Action Report*, 2013.

FEMA. *National Urban Search and Rescue Strategic Plan 2013-2017* 2013.

FEMA. "About the Agency" http://www.fema.gov/about-agency (accessed March 2014).

Fetterman, David M. *Ethnography*. Vol. 17. Second ed. Applied Social Research Methods Series. Thousand Oaks, CA: SAGE Publications, 1998.

Follett, Mary Parker. "The Giving of Orders." In *Classics of Public Administration*, edited by Jay M. Schafritz and Albert C. Hyde, 53-60. Fort Worth, TX: Harcourt Brace, 1926.

Fraser, Douglas M. Usaf and Wendell S. Usaf Hertzelle. "Haiti Relief: An International Effort Enabled through Air, Space, and Cyberspace." *Air & Space Power Journal* 24, no. 4 (2010): 5-12.

Freidson, Eliot. *Professional Powers*. Chicago, IL: University of Chicago Press, 1986.

Freidson, Eliot. *Professionalism: The Third Logic*. Chicago, IL: The University of Chicago Press, 2001.

Frontline. *After the Storm*. Public Broadcasting System, 2005.

GAO. *Coast Guard: Observations on the Preparation, Response, and Recovery Missions Related to Hurricane Katrina*, 2006. GAO-06-903.

GAO. *U.S. Southern Command Demonstrates Interagency Collaboration, but Its Haiti Disaster Response Revealed Challenges Conducting a Large Military Operation*, 2010.

REFERENCES

Geisel, Harold W. *Review of the Department of State Interagencu Coordination and Public Communications Regarding U.S. Citizen Victims in the Earthquake Destroyed Hotel Montana in Haiti*, 2010.

Global Security, "US Military Operations in Haiti" http://www.globalsecurity.org/military/ops/haiti.htm (accessed August 2013).

Guha-Sapir, Debarati, Thomas Kirsch, Shayna Dooling, Adam Sirois and Maral DerSarkissian. *Independent Review of the U.S. Government Response to the Haiti Earthquake*, 2011. AID-OAA-TO-10-00020.

Gulick, Luther. "Notes on the Theory of Organization." In *Classics of Public Administration*. Fort Worth, TX: Harcourt Brace College Publishers, 1937.

Hamner, Marvine P. "Organizational Transformation: Impact of Redesigning the American Red Cross Disaster Services Human Resource System." *Journal of Homeland Security and Emergency Management* 5, no. 1 (2008).

Harrald, John R. "Agility and Discipline: Critical Success Factors for Disaster Response." *Annals of the American Academy of Political and Social Science* 604,(2006): 256-272.

Hogue, Henry B. and Keith Bea. *Federal Emergency Management and Homeland Security Organization: Historical Developments and Legislative Options*, 2006.

Homeland Security National Preparedness Task Force. *Civil Defense and Homeland Security: A Short History of National Preparedness Efforts*, 2006.

Huntington, Samuel P. *The Soldier and the State*. New York: Vintage Books, 1957.

Joint Center for Operational Analysis. *Operation Unified Response Haiti Earthquake Response*, 2010.

Joint Center for Operational Analysis. *Humanitarian Assistance and Disaster Relief Lessons Information Paper*, 2011.

Johnson, Linda M. "U.S. Coast Guard's HC-144A Supports Haitian Relief Operations, Service Plans to Purchase Additional Aircraft." *Delivering the Goods: News from the US Coast Guard Acquisition Directorate*, February 2010.

Kaufman, Herbert. *The Forest Ranger: A Study in Administrative Behavior*. Johns Hopkins University Press, 1960.

Keane, Thomas H. "The 9/11 Commission Report." In *The National Commission on Terrorist Attacks Upon the United States*. Washington, DC: W.W. Norton & Company, 2002.

REFERENCES

Keen, P.K., Matthew G. Elledge, Charles W. Nolan and Jennifer L. Kimmey. "Foreign Disaster Response: Joint Task Force Haiti Observations." *Military Review*, (2010): 85-96.

Keelean, Dan. *Informing FEMA's Future Workforce Strategy: FEMA Strategic Workforce Initiative Phase II*, Homeland Security Studies and Analysis Institute, 2012.

Kettl, D.F. "Contingent Coordination: Practical and Theoretical Puzzles for Homeland Security." *American Review Of Public Administration* 33, no. 3 (2003): 253-277.

Khademian, Anne M. *Working with Culture: The Way the Job Gets Done in Public Programs*. Washington, DC: CQ Press, 2002.

Klapper, Matt and James J. Riley. "Haiti Lessons: A Search and Rescue Corps..." *The New York Times*, February 13, 2010.

Klein, Gary and Beth Crandall. *Recognition-Primed Decision Strategies*, 1996.

Koch, Mitchell T. "HA/DR Lessons Learned." Naval War College, 2011.

Kraska, Peter B. "Enjoying Militarism: Political/Personal Dilemmas in Studying U.S. Police Paramilitary Units." *Justice quarterly* 13, no. 3 (1996): 405.

Kraska, Peter B. and Victor E. Kappeler. "Militarizing American Police: The Rise and Normalization of Paramilitary Units." *Social Problems* 44, no. 1 (1997): 1-18.

Kreps, Gary A. "The Organization of Disaster Response: Core Concepts and Principals." In *Tenth World Congress of Sociology*. Mexico City, MX, 1982.

Kreps, Gary A. "Description, Taxonomy, and Explanation in Disaster Research." *International Journal of Mass Emergencies and Disasters* 7, no. 3 (1989): 277-280.

Kreps, Gary. "Disaster as Systemic Event and Social Catalyst: A Clarification of Subject Matter." *International Journal of Mass Emergencies and Disasters* 13, no. 3 (1995): 255-285.

Kreps, Gary A. and Thomas E. Drabek. "Disasters Are Nonroutine Social Problems." *International Journal of Mass Emergencies and Disasters* 14, no. 2 (1996): 129-153.

Langston, Thomas S. "The Civilian Side of Military Culture." *Parameters*, (2000): 21-29.

Legeros, Mike. "FEMA Summary of USAR Activations for Haiti Earthquake". 2010.

Leonard, Herman B. "Dutch" and Arnold M. Howitt. "The Heat of the Moment." *Compass*, Fall 2004, 18-23.

Leonard, Herman and Arn Howitt. "Rethinking the Management of Large Scale National Emergencies." In *Acting in Time Against Landscape Scale Disasters*. Geneva, SU, 2012.

Leonard, Herman and Arnold Howitt. "High Performance in Emergency Preparedness and Response: Disaster Type Differences." 8. Cambridge, MA: Harvard University A. Alfred Taubman Center for State and Local Government, 2007.

Lewis, David E. *The Politics of Presidential Appointmets: Political Control and Bureacratic Performance*: Princeton University Press, 2008.

Lipsky, Michael. *Street-Level Bureaucracy: Dilemmas of the Individual in Public Service, 30th Anniversary Expanded Edition*: Russell Sage Foundation, 2010.

Lipton, Eric. "Devastation, Seen from a Ship." *The New York Times*, January 13, 2010.

Lofton, Lisa. *Haiti Earthquake Response Quick Look Report*, 2010.

Lutz, Catherine. "Making War at Home in the United States: Militarization and the Current Crisis." *American Anthropologist* 104, no. 3 (2002): 723-735.

Luu, Ky, "Ken Keen Interview", Disaster Resilience Leadership Academy http://www.drlatulane.org/leadership-corner/interviews/ken-keen-interview (accessed March 13, 2014).

Mandeles, Mark D. "Imposing Order on Chaos: Establishing JTF Headquarters." *Joint Center for Operational Analysis Journal* XII, no. 2 (2010): 21-32.

Mahoney, James. 2010. "After KKV: The New Methodology of Qualitative Research." *World Politics* 62 (1): 120–47.

Marcus, L. J., B. C. Dorn and J. M. Henderson. "Meta-Leadership and National Emergency Preparedness: A Model to Build Government Connectivity." *Biosecurity and Bioterrorism-Biodefense Strategy Practice and Science* 4, no. 2 (2006): 128-134.

Marcus, Leonard J., Isaac Ashkenazi, Barry C. Dorn and Joseph M. Henderson. "National Preparedness and the Five Dimensions of Meta-Leadership." Cambridge, MA: National Preparedness Leadership Initiative at Harvard University 2007.

Martin, David. *Bringing the Military's Might to Haiti*. CBS News, 2010.

McReynolds, William H. "The Office for Emergency Management." *Public Administration Review* 1, no. 2 (1941): 131-138.

Miles, Matthew B. and A. Michael Huberman. *Qualitative Data Analysis: A Sourcebook of New Methods*. Beverly Hills, CA: SAGE Publications, 1984.

Morrissey, Siobhan. "The Coast Guard in Haiti: First Responders in for the Long Haul." *Time*, January 22 2010.

Morton, John. *Next-Generation Homeland Security: Network Federalism and the Course to National Preparedness*: Naval Institute Press, 2012.

REFERENCES

Muggah, Robert. "The Effects of Stabliisation on Humanitarian Action in Haiti." *Disasters* 34, no. S3 (2010): 444-463.

Munsing, Evan and Christopher J. Lamb. *Joint Interagency Task Force–South: The Best Known, Least Understood Interagency Success.* Washington, DC: Institute for National Strategic Studies, National Defense University, 2011.

Murray, Williamson. "Military Culture Does Matter." *Orbis* 7, no. 2 (1999).

Nagl, John A. and Elizabeth O. Young. "Si Vis Pacem, Para Pacem: Training for Humanitarian Emergencies." *Military Review* 80, no. 2 (2000).

NAPA. *FEMA's Integration of Preparedness and Development of Robust Regional Offices: an Independent Assessment.* Washington, DC: National Academy for Public Administration, 2009.

Nash, Roy. "Help and Hope for Haiti." *The Coast Guard Journal of Safety and Security at Sea* 67, no. 2 (2010): 50-78.

Neal, David M. "The Local Red Cross in Time of Disaster: Characteristics and Conditions of Organizational Effectiveness During the Loma Prieta Earthquake and Central Texas Floods." *The Journal of Volunteer Administration* 11, no. 2 (1992): 6-16.

Neal, David M. and Brenda D. Phillips. "Effective Emergency Management: Reconsidering the Bureaucratic Approach." *Disasters* 19, no. 4 (1995): 327-337.

Nisbet, Robert and Jo Couzens. *US Troops Pour in to Boost Quake Op.* London, UK: Sky News, 2010.

NOAA, "Preliminary Info on 2012 U.S. Billion-Dollar Extreme Weather/Climate Events", National Climate Data Center http://www.ncdc.noaa.gov/news/preliminary-info-2012-us-billion-dollar-extreme-weatherclimate-events (accessed November 22 2013).

Nolte, Isabella M. and Silke Boenigk. "Public-Nonprofit Partnership Performance in a Disaster Context: The Case of Haiti." *Public Administration* 89, (2011): 1385-1402.

Nolte, Isabella M. and Silke Boenigk. "A Study of Ad Hoc Network Performance in Disaster Response." *Nonprofit and Voluntary Sector Quarterly* 42, no. 1 (2013): 148-173.

NRC. *Tools and Methods for Estimating Populations at Risk from Natural Disasters and Complex Humanitarian Crises,* 2007.

Obama, Barack. *Presidential Policy Directive 8: National Preparedness,* 2011.

REFERENCES

Odeen, Philip, Yvonne B. Burke, Frank C. Carlucci, Charles L. Dempsey, Thomas M. Downs, Andrew J. Goodpaster, Stan M. McKinney, Elmer B. Staats and Lee M. Thomas. *Coping with Catastrophe: Building and Emergency Management System to Meet People's Needs in Natural and Manmade Disasters*. Washington, DC: National Academy of Public Administration, 1993, EMW-930C-4097.

Olafsson, Gisli Rafn. "Effective Coordination of Disaster Response: The International Perspective." In *7th International ISCRAM Conference*. Seattle, WA, 2010.

Olsen, Lise. "5 Years after Katrina, Storm's Death Toll Remains a Mystery." *Houston Chronicle*, August 30 2010.

Parkyn, Michael. "Analytic Support for FEMA Disaster Operations: Training Review and Way Forward." FEMA Response Directorate. Washington, DC: Homeland Security Studies and Anysis Institute, 2011.

Petak, William J. *Emergency Management: A Challenge for Public Administration*. Washington, DC, 1985.

Poirier, Alfred. "FEMA Urban Search and Rescue Teams: Considering an Improved Strategy for an Evolving Homeland Security Enterprise " Naval Postgraduate School, 2012.

Quarantelli, E.L. *Inventory of Disaster Field Studies in the Social and Behavioral Sciences 1919–1979*. University of Delaware, 1982.

Reilly, Jim. "Thunderbolt Exercises Helped Florida React During Blackout." *Emergency Management*, January 14 2009.

REUTERS. "Death Toll Rises to 92 in School Collapse in Haiti " *The New York Times*, November 8, 2008.

Richards, Anne L. *Annual Review of the United States Coast Guard's Mission Performance (FY 2010)*, 2011.

Ripley, Amanda. "In Case of Emergency." *The Atlantic*, September 1, 2009.

Roberts, Patrick S. *Disasters and the American State: How Politicians, Bureaucrats, and the Public Prepare for the Unexpected*. New York, NY Cambridge University Press, 2013.

Roberts, Patrick. "Private Choices, Public Harms: The Evolution of National Disaster Organizations in the United States." In *Disaster and the Politics of Intervention*. New York: Columbia Unversity Press, 2010.

Roberts, Patrick S. "FEMA and Prospects for Reputation-Based Autonomy." *Studies in American Political Development* 20, no. 1 (2006).

Rodriguez, Havidan, Enrico L. Quarantelli and Russel R. Dynes, eds. *Handbook of Disaster Research*. New York: Springer Science+Business Media, LLC, 2007.

REFERENCES

Rohter, Larry. "Pentagon Shifts Its Caribbean Command to Aid in Drug Fight " *The New York Times*, June 8 1997.

Roig-Farnzia, Manuel, Mary Beth Sheridan and Michael E. Ruane. "Security Fears Mount in Lawless Post-Earthquake Haiti." *The Washington Post*, January 18 2010.

Rosen, Stephen Peter. "Military Effectiveness: Why Society Matters." *International Security* 19, no. 4 (1995): 5-31.

Rubin, Claire. *Emergency Management: The American Experience 1900-2010*. Second ed. Boca Raton, FL: Taylor & Francis Group, 2012.

Ruisi, Anne. "Body of Birmingham Native Ken Bourland Recovered in Haiti." *The Birmingham News*, February 8 2010.

Ryan, John, Russ Goehring and Robert Hulslander. "Us Southcom Ad Joint Task Force-Haiti… Some Challenges and Considerations in Forming a Joint Task Force." *Joint Center for Operational Analysis Journal* XII, no. 2 (2010).

Schein, Edgar H. *Organizational Culture and Leadership*. San Francisco: Jossey-Bass, 2004.

Small, David, "Airman Named to Time Magazine's 100 Most Influential People List for Haitian Airfield Efforts", SOUTHCOM http://www.southcom.mil/newsroom/Pages/Airman-named-to-Time-Magazine%27s-%27100-most-influential-people%27-list-for-Haiti-airfield-efforts.aspx (accessed April 3 2014).

SOUTHCOM, "Biography Lieutenant General PK Keen" http://usacac.army.mil/cac2/AOKM/aokm2009/bio/Keen_PK_LTG_Bio.pdf (accessed March 24 2014).

SOUTHCOM, "Contingency Response, Disaster Relief, Humanitarian Assistance" http://www.southcom.mil/ourmissions/Pages/Contingency-Response--Disaster-Relief--Humanitarian-Assistance-.aspx (accessed April 3 2014).

SOUTHCOM, "History" http://www.southcom.mil/aboutus/Pages/History.aspx (accessed April 3 2014).

SOUTHCOM, "Missions" http://www.southcom.mil/ourmissions/Pages/Our-Missions.aspx (accessed April 3 2014).

SOUTHCOM, "Operation Unified Response: Support to Haiti Earthquake Relief 2010" http://www.southcom.mil/newsroom/Pages/Operation-Unified-Response-Support-to-Haiti-Earthquake-Relief-2010.aspx (accessed April 3 2014).

Stallings, Robert A., ed. *Methods of Disaster Research*: International Research Committee on Disasters, 2002.

Stephenson, Max O. and Laura Zanotti. *Peacebuilding through Community Based NGOs: Paradoxes and Possibilties*. Sterling, VA: Stylus Publishing LLC, 2012.

Strauss, Anselm and Juliet Corbin. *Basics of Qualitative Research: Techniques and Procedures for Developing Grounded Theory*. 2nd ed. Thousand Oaks, CA: Sage Publications, 1998.

Sylves, Richard. "Ferment at FEMA: Reforming Emergency Management." *Public Administration Review* 54, no. 3 (1994): 303-307.

Sylves, Richard. *Disaster Policy and Politics: Emergency Management and Homeland Security*. Washington, DC: CQ Press, 2009.

Tamargo, Timothy. 2011. "Coast Guard Cutter Commander Shares Haitian Earthquake Experience," http://coastguardnews.com/coast-guard-cutter-commander-shares-haiti-experience/2011/04/07/ (accessed July 2013).

Tan, Michelle. "82nd Tackles Grf, Relearns Rapid Deployment." *Army Times*, May 22, 2013.

Tanner, Robert and Jennifer Loven. "The Cavalry Arrives but Refugees and Local Officials Want to Know Why It Took So Long." *Associated Press*, September 3, 2005.

Thompson, Bennie. *Redirecting FEMA Towards Success*, 2006.

Thompson, DeniseD P. "Leveraging Learning to Improve Disaster Management Outcomes." *International Journal of Disaster Risk Science* 3, no. 4 (2012): 195-206.

Tierney, Kathleen and Christine Bevc. "Disaster as War: Militarism Andthe Social Construction of Disaster in New Orleans." In *The Sociology of Katrina: Perspectives on a Modern Catastrophe*, edited by David L. Brusnma, 37-54. Lanham, MD: Rowman & Littlefield, 2010.

Tolbert, Pamela S. and Lynne G. Zucker. "Institutional Sources of Change in the Formal Structure of Organizations: The Diffusion of Civil Service Reform, 1880-1935." *Administrative Science Quarterly* 28, no. 1 (1983): 22-39.

Townsend, Frances Frago. *The Federal Response to Hurricane Katrina: Lessons Learned*. Washington, DC: The White House Homeland Security Council, 2006.

Trice, Harrison and Janice Beyer. *The Cultures of Work Organizations*: Prentice Hall, 1993.

United Nations. *Disaster Preparedness for Effective Response Guidance and Indicator Package for Implementing Priority Five of the Hyogo Framework Hyogo Framework for Action 2005-2015: Building the Resilience of Nations and Communities to Ddisasters*, 2008.

United Nations. "Disaster Impact 2000-2012." UN Office for Disaster Risk Reduction, 2013.

REFERENCES

United Nations. *Global Assessment Report on Disaster Risk Reduction*, 2013.

United Nations. "Mission Des Nations Unies Pour La Stabilisation En Haïti" http://www.un.org/en/peacekeeping/missions/minustah/ (accessed August 2013).

United Nations. "Un Cluster System" http://business.un.org/en/documents/249 (accessed September 2013).

USAID, "Swearing in of Rajiv Shah" http://www.usaid.gov/who-we-are/organization/rajiv-shah (accessed September 2013).

USAID, "USAID Urban Search and Rescue Teams from Los Angeles and Fairfax Counties Train First-Responders in Haiti" http://www.usaid.gov/content/usaid-urban-search-and-rescue-teams-los-angeles-and-fairfax-counties-train-first-responders (accessed April 1 2014).

US Army, "Ken Keen Biographical Information" http://usacac.army.mil/cac2/AOKM/aokm2009/bio/Keen_PK_LTG_Bio.pdf (accessed December 2013).

USCG. *Leadership Development Framework*, 2006. COMDTINST M5351.3.

USCG. *U.S. Coast Guard Incident Management Handbook*, 2006.

USCG. *U.S. Coast Guard International Training Handbook*, 2008.

USCG. *U.S. Coast Guard Publication 1: America's Maritime Guardian*, 2009.

USCG. *Secretary Napolitano Authorizes Activation of Reserve Coast Guard Personnel to Support Efforts in Haiti*, 2010.

USCG. *Deepwater Horizon ISPR Final Report*, 2011.

USCG, "U.S. Coast Guard Disaster History" http://www.uscg.mil/history/disastersindex.asp (accessed August 2013).

USCG, "U.S. Coast Guard History" http://www.uscg.mil/history/ (accessed August 2013).

USCG, "U.S. Coast Guard Initial Training" http://www.gocoastguard.com/find-your-career/reserve-opportunities/reserve-officer-opportunities/initial-training (accessed August 2013).

USGS, "Richter Scale", Department of Interior http://earthquake.usgs.gov/learn/topics/richter.php (accessed August 2013).

USGS, "Earthquake Alerting System" http://earthquake.usgs.gov/earthquakes/feed/v1.0/ (accessed January 2014).

US House of Representatives. *A Failure of Initiative*. Washington, DC: US House of
    Representatives Select Bipartisan Committee to Investigate the Preparation for and
    Response to Hurricane Katrina, 2006.

Van Evera, Stephen. 1997. *Guide to Methods for Students of   Political Science*. Ithaca, NY:
Cornell University   Press.

VA-TF1. *USA-1/VA-TF1 Urban Search and Rescue Response to the 2010 Haiti Earthquake*.
    Fairfax, VA, 2010.

Wamsley, Gary. *The Role of the National Guard in Emergency Preparedness and Response*.
    Washington, DC, 1997.

Wamsley, Gary L. "Contrasting Institutions of Air Force Specializatoin: Happenstance or
    Bellweather." *American Journal of Sociology* 78, no. 2 (1972): 399-417.

Wamsley, Gary L. "Escalating in a Quagmire: The Changing Dynamics of the Emergency
    Management Policy Subsystem." *Public Administration Review* 56, no. 3 (1996): 235-
    244.

Waugh, William L. and Gregory Streib. "Collaboration and Leadership for Effective
    Emergency Management." *Public Administration Review* 66, (2006): 131-140.

Weber, Max. "Bureaucracy." In *Essays in Sociology*. Oxford, England: Oxford University Press,
    1946.

Weick, Karl E. "The Collapse of Sensemaking in Organizations: The Mann Gulch Disaster."
    Administrative Science Quarterly 38, no. 4 (1993): 628-652.

Weisenfeld, Paul E. "Successes and Challenges of the Haiti Earthquake Response: The
    Experience of USAID." *Emory International Law Review* 25, (2011): 1098-1120.

Wheeler, Carol McBryde, Penny Pennington Weeks and Diane Montgomery. "Disaster
    Response Leadership: Perceptions of American Red Cross Workers." *International
    Journal of Leadership Studies* 8, no. 1 (2013): 79-100.

Wilson, James Q. *Bureaucracy: What Government Agencies Do and Why They Do It*: Harper Collins
    Publishers, 1989.

Wilson, Peter. "Defining Military Culture." *The Journal of Military History* 72, (2007): 11-41.

Wolbers, Jeroen and Kees Boersma. "The Common Operational Picture as Collective
    Sensemaking." *Journal of Contingencies and Crisis Management* 21, no. 4 (2013).

Yin, Robert K. *Case Study Research: Design and Methods*. Vol. 5. 3rd ed. Applied Social Research
    Methods Series. Thousand Oaks, CA: Sage Publications, 2003.

REFERENCES

Zanotti, Laura. "Cacophonies of Aid, Failed State Building and NGOs in Haiti: Setting the Stage for Disaster, Envisioning the Future." *Third World Quarterly* 31, no. 5 (2010): 755-771.

APPENDIX A.

APPENDIX A: LIST OF INTERVIEWEES

Captain Doug Fears, U.S. Coast Guard, Commanding Officer, USCGC *Hamilton*
August 22, 2013

Corey Coleman, FEMA Chief Human Capital Officer
September 6, 2013

Chief R. David Paulison, former FEMA Administrator
October 15, 2013

Mike Byrne, American Red Cross & former FEMA National Incident Management
Assistance Team Leader
October 15, 2013

Richard Reed, Senior Vice President, American Red Cross & former Deputy Assistant to the
President for Homeland Security, The White House
October 16, 2013

Admiral Tom Atkin (ret.), U.S. Coast Guard
October 21, 2013

Chief Jack Brown (ret.), U.S. Coast Guard & Director of Emergency Management, Arlington
County, Virginia
October 22, 2013

Admiral Thad Allen (ret.), former Commandant, U.S. Coast Guard
October 24, 2013

Colonel Chuck Donnell (ret.), U.S. Army & American Red Cross
October 28, 2013

Admiral Harvey Johnson (ret.), U.S. Coast Guard & former FEMA Deputy Administrator
November 4, 2013

Tim Manning, Deputy Administrator of FEMA for Protection and National Preparedness
December 11, 2013

Major General Steve Saunders (ret.), National Guard & FEMA Executive Director of
Readiness and Assessment
December 13, 2013

David Kaufman, FEMA Associate Administrator for Policy, Program Analysis, and
International Affairs
December 20, 2013

103

Colonel Damon Penn (ret.), U.S. Army & FEMA Assistant Administrator of the National Continuity Programs
December 23, 2013

Debra "D.J." Sessner, FEMA Readiness & Assessment Program and FEMA National Incident Management Assistance Team-West
January 14, 2014

Captain Rick Morrison (ret.), U.S. Navy and member, FEMA Doctrine Development Team, Homeland Security Studies and Analysis Institute
January 29, 2014

Captain Diane W. Durham, U.S. Coast Guard, Commanding Officer USCGC *Rush*
March 20, 2014

Battalion Chief Kathleen Stanley, Fairfax County Fire & Rescue Department, Rescue Specialist, Virginia Task Force 1 Urban Search and Rescue (VATF-1)
March 27, 2014

Lieutenant Colonel J. Parks Hughes, former Squadron Commander, 21st Special Tactics Squadron, 720th Special Tactics Group, U.S. Air Force Special Operations Command
April 1, 2014